Managing
Screen Time

Translated by Eduard van der Maas

First published in Dutch as *Beeldscherm beelden* by
Uitgeverij Christofoor in 2015
Published in English by Floris Books in 2016
© 2015 Edmond Schoorel/Uitgeverij Christofoor
English version © 2016 Floris Books

Also available
as an eBook

MIX
Paper from
responsible sources
FSC® C007785

British Library CIP data available
ISBN 978-178250-248-7
Printed in Great Britian
by Bell and Bain Ltd

Managing Screen Time

Raising balanced children
in the digital age

Edmond Schoorel

Floris
Books

Contents

Prelude

Who am I? Who are you?

Dear Reader,

Let me begin with a question: Who are you? To answer this, let's start by thinking about how you were raised. After all, we're partly a product of our upbringing. What role did electronic and digital media play in your upbringing? How much do you owe to television, telephones, the internet, social media, the apps on your iPhone or tablet? Or did your parents, and perhaps your teachers and friends, have a stronger influence on you?

The best way to look closely at who you really are is to look back at who played a key role in your upbringing. To do this effectively, it helps to ask this question as if you were an involved outsider, rather than the insider that you are. Perhaps you find you learned a lot from one particular teacher but very little from another. Try again, this time without sympathy or disapproval. What did you really *learn* from this person? Which part of you has become the way you are because of this person?

After you have tried this mentally with a few people, look in this same way at television and digital media. Do you notice a similar influence? Television and (depending on your age) digital media have probably played an enormous role in your upbringing. They have determined, in part, who you are.

How do you think today's kids will answer this question? Some children in the West devote more time to digital media than to sleeping and eating – and much more time than to school and homework. Adults in the West spend more time looking into the eyes of television stars than into those of their own partner. Many parents have given up trying to know with whom and with what their kids are in contact in the digital world. Children raise one another – that was always the case; children are being raised by digital media – that is new.

If you're comfortable with the fact that our children and grandchildren, students and clients are being raised by digital media, please read on. I will show you an additional task that's required in parenting: a job you cannot leave to the media but will have to manage yourself, namely allowing children to become themselves as human beings.

If you feel uncomfortable with the fact that modern children are increasingly being raised via screens large and small, please read on. You're right: there are serious side effects. And if children are to become themselves, we need to include an extra task in our parenting to combat these side effects, a challenge as new as the screens themselves.

It's not a case of reacting against the mainstream, as Rudolf Steiner and Ita Wegman wrote in their basic book on anthroposophical medicine.[1] Anthroposophy aims to offer perspectives that broaden the field of study, while not detracting from the value of accepted medicine (and other disciplines).

This is also true of modern developments surrounding the digitisation of society. We live in a digital age and we can gratefully make use of the possibilities this offers. But nothing should prevent us from facing the side effects of digital media or from taking the necessary measures to neutralise them.

In the first four chapters of this book I outline the effects of digitisation in our world. The world has changed, people have changed, the role of parents has changed – and all of this with great speed and astonishing pervasiveness. The consequences are significant and to a large extent cannot yet be foreseen. Digital media play a role in the formative process of becoming human beings. Millions of people are the way they are as a result of the influence of television, computers, tablets, smartphones, and so forth. Millions experience problems as a result: headaches, shoulder and neck complaints, obesity, stress, sleeping problems, loneliness, aggression and memory loss.

Surely no one would choose these complaints voluntarily? So why does it happen? What interests are at work in the world of multimedia? Chapters 5 to 9 deal with the questions: What lies behind this phenomenon?

What's actually happening? I try to answer by exploring the themes of *image* and *virtual*.

The final chapters contain advice – both for those who are comfortable with our modern use of digital media and for those with a more critical attitude.

Chapter 1.
How Digital Media
Are Changing the World

Whatever happened to the friendly paperboy, who cheerfully passed the time of day while delivering newspapers? This role has largely been relegated to the realm of nostalgia. Even personal letters have been replaced by emails and our letterbox replaced by an inbox, containing dozens of emails each day that we don't have time to read. When we go on holiday we can ask neighbours to make sure our letterbox doesn't get clogged up. At least this encourages us to talk to our neighbours for once. Fortunately we can programme our electronic mailbox to automatically delete emails.

We no longer need newspapers to be delivered to our door. Within a few minutes, or at most a few hours, we can be abreast of everything that's going on in the world – especially if there was a microphone or camera nearby, which is almost always the case, because any self-respecting mobile phone today has both. When we're listening to the radio or surfing the internet, sounds and sights from the other side of the world force themselves upon us. The news finds us; we don't have to look for it.

Of course, we can't be aware of everything that happens in the world. But who determines which events from our 'global village'[2] arrive on our doorstep? We can choose the TV channel, radio station or website, which makes some difference, at least to the tone in which reports are presented: biased or neutral, in depth or brief, with or without background music. But do we have a real understanding of why there are reporters in certain parts of the world and not in others?

And how much news can we bear? We see and hear other people's misery, we want to help, we want to *do* something, but how? We can send money to charities providing relief in Syria, Afghanistan, Sudan, Gaza or Ukraine. A drop in the ocean, the realist in us says. Or we can do battle on the *right* side, says our inner crusader. Or shall we pray for them, for all those perpetrators and victims and the families of perpetrators and victims? Then we'd be praying all day long. Or should everyone solve their own problems and seek peace and justice in their own small world, the best they can?

The 'global village' has enormous consequences for our moral choices. Digital media, especially social media, have been decisive in the dissemination of social revolutions and popular revolts all around the world. The election of Obama as President of the USA, the overthrow of old regimes in North Africa and the rise of the so-called Islamic State in Iraq are examples of this. Who would have imagined we could contribute to such worldwide events and movements from our own doorstep.

Infrastructure

The earth has acquired a different complexion. How romantically charming old telephone wires and electricity lines now seem, although they were, of course, also products of a technological culture. But they 'stand' in the landscape. Swallows and sparrows give them an almost photogenic appearance. Wind Turbines and huge modern pylons are by comparison horizon-polluting junk, and there have been claims that they can impose a risk to the health of those that live nearby to them.

Wherever possible we have put electric cables under the ground, out of sight. There they lie next to sewers, which take our waste to treatment plants. Once in a while when the street is dug up for the umpteenth time so the umpteenth provider can put its cables next to the rest, we can see how many pipes and cables lie underground. Imagine a map of our country showing all the sewers, pipes and cables: that would give us a clearer sense of what the earth has to endure from all our waste and information streams.

And it's the same above ground. Transmission masts have been erected in strategic locations to guarantee that everybody has 'signal' everywhere. Church steeples are also used as masts, serving a new, secularised purpose. Imagine what our world would look like if we had a map of all the invisible signals and carrier waves! The whole world would be encompassed by a gigantic spider's web. We can't see this web, but it is there, and it has transformed the appearance of the world. It confuses migratory birds, disturbing their long-standing routes.

Electricity

Anyone who has experienced a power cut lasting a few hours will realise to what extent our lives depend on electricity. Without electric lights we can no longer extend the day and push back the night. An entire neighbourhood or city without light feels ominous; it attracts thieves, and anxiety creeps into the soul.

Without electricity, not only are the lights extinguished, but the heating and refrigerator also stop working. Some people may have a wood-burning stove or an open fireplace, and food will keep for a few hours in the freezer and refrigerator with the doors closed, but not for long. Our first instinct may be to check our power supplier's website to see when they expect the problem to be resolved – but the computer doesn't work either. We may choose not to use up precious battery power on our phone, tablet or laptop for a while because who knows when we'll really need it.

It's only when we stop to think about the number of things in our lives that are powered by electricity that we realise to what extent this great achievement of humankind has penetrated our daily lives. How would our lives change if we were without electricity for a week or a month? What would we do, what would remain of our way of life?

It's hard to imagine how people existed for so many centuries without electricity. Great works of art were created before the discovery of electricity. Would these works of art have been created if people had electricity back then? But that is art-from-then – what is art-from-now? Video installations? Karlheinz Stockhausen's Helicopter String Quartet, which involves musicians and pilots in four helicopters, audio and video technicians and equipment?

Information

How did people find out information before the internet existed? This is probably an easy question for you, but will your children know, or your grandchildren? Before the internet, we learned through direct conversations with people more knowledgeable or experienced than ourselves, and in doing so we not only found out the facts we were looking for, but also something about our teachers' lives: how they had gained their knowledge and how they had applied it.

For a great many centuries people have had the irrepressible impulse to write down what they have experienced, learned or imagined in the form of books. Libraries came into being, where people who were able to read could become acquainted with the knowledge and experience of others.

The invention of the printing press brought with it a huge development in the history of learning, making printed copies of books available to all those who could read. Many more people then learned to read and write and the Western world quickly became literate. Reading books and therefore gaining knowledge meant conquering the world. A country's literacy rate became a measure of its levels of civilisation, influence and power. Knowledge became power and the library it's admission ticket.

These days our trips to the library are less common – although libraries still provide a wonderful resource for people of all ages and from all walks of life. We tend to buy books or borrow them from one another, not from the library, and we are much less inclined to go to the library to find out information. Instead we turn on the computer and ask a search engine, in most cases Google. The worldwide proliferation of Google is so extensive that 'to google' has become a verb in itself. Whatever we're searching for, Google will find a range of websites, which may or may not provide relevant information. How Google searches, and why certain answers stand at the top of the list, only Google knows. It has something to do with money; that much is certain. It seems like our search doesn't cost anything but, of course, that's not true. We don't immediately pay a fee, but our mouse-clicks make us objects of research and our search in itself becomes merchandise.

For example, if we search a few times for 'temples in Greece', we will receive advertisements and offers from hotels in Greece, probably that same day. This indicates an important shift in the provision of information. The primary purpose of our modern library, the search engine, is not to provide correct information, but to record our behaviour in order to generate income.

Information delivered by a search engine also differs from books and direct conversations in another respect: good books and teachers can deliver the context of the information, whereas many of the websites gathered by a search engine can, out of context, be confusing.

Developmental steps

All the key steps in the development of humanity have changed the landscape of our world. Let me mention a few.

Fire

The use of fire brought humanity from the Stone Age to the Iron Age. By using fire, people could extract iron and other metals from various kinds of rock. The increased sophistication of tools and decorative objects was enormous. People could develop skills that, until now, had been out of reach. By developing these skills people themselves changed: their motor skills, physique, mentality and brains adapted. This process applies both to individuals and to humanity as a whole: we are shaped by what we do and by what we don't do.

The wheel

The invention of the wheel, or rather the invention of two wheels with an axle between them, meant that people spent considerably less time walking. Thousands of people have travelled across the earth on their feet. During the early human migrations they travelled improbably great distances. They discovered the earth on foot, and came to know its hardness and softness through the soles of their feet: we could say this is how the earth and people came to know each other. Wheels brought about a huge revolution. Pulling wagons and similar exhausting work could be outsourced to animals. Human beings could 'make better use' of their energy. The price they paid was becoming further removed from the earth. The gain, conversely, was that they acquired a higher and freer position for gathering knowledge about the earth.

Printing

We have already mentioned the invention of printing – an enormous step forward in the development of so many people – but it did exact a price. Before printed books were available people had to rely on memory to know, for example, the history of their people, which was preserved in the nation's collective memory through incredibly long epic tales. Memory is one of the central functions of the self: without it we are nowhere and nobody. Over the course of a few generations our powers of memory withered. Outsourcing our narratives from collective memory to books has thoroughly changed humankind. The gain: individual consciousness that is up to date and topical. The loss: historical consciousness – the awareness of being part of development, embedded in the flow of time.

The Industrial Revolution

In the latter decades of the eighteenth century, large machines were invented to carry out work that had previously been done with tools. First came steam engines, huge monsters that could withstand the high pressure produced by steam. Even today we are fascinated by the heat and steam produced by these machines, the clearly visible way they function, the sound and power generated, and the way that power is transferred. Then followed smaller and more compact diesel and gasoline engines, in which the mechanism is more hidden and the power generated not as obvious.

A new era dawned in which manual labourers were freed from back-breaking physical exertion. As a result, thousands of people became unemployed. Their strength was transferred to the machines as 'horsepower', miraculously provided by the ingenuity of engineers. The energy thus released, the man-hours saved, could be used for a higher purpose: the intellectual and cultural formation of people. This did happen, and we would surely never wish to reverse the gain in knowledge the whole populace acquired in this way. But there were also, unavoidably, side effects. Skilled knowledge, for example in weaving and dying cloth, was lost. Industry moved to regions close to cities and turned them into unhealthy places with unparalleled environmental pressures, new social inequalities, poverty and alcohol abuse.

Every invention that replaces a task previously done by people has this effect: it brings something new and takes something away. This also applies to small things, such as press studs and Velcro. Check the devices around you to see how this effect applies to them. The digital revolution is no small matter. It's a revolution for the world, for humanity, and for all the beings who inhabit the earth.

An Interlude on Child Development: The Fourfold Human Being

There is a very useful classification for describing the many different processes that take place within us. I derive this classification from anthroposophy[1], but it's also described in other cultures and social movements. In this classification people consist of four levels:

1. the physical level (body)
2. the level of life functions, the metabolic processes (body)
3. the level of the soul (soul)
4. the level of the self or spirit (soul)

This classification dovetails with the body-soul polarity, which has been elaborated, for example, in psychosomatic medicine. The first two levels (the physical level and the life functions) belong to the 'body'; the second two levels (the soul and the self) belong to the 'soul'. In this concept the two aspects of body and soul are essential for each of us. If all is well, we identify with both our body and our soul. There is no misunderstanding about the difference between body and soul. But it is quite different when it comes to the two parts of body and the two parts of soul respectively. Here we can easily encounter misunderstanding. The difference between the body and the life within that body calls for explanation, as does the difference between the soul and the self or spirit.

The *physical* level and that of our *life processes* can easily be swept into one pile. In medical training they are actually two fields of study: anatomy and physiology. But in textbooks this distinction disappears again: physiological processes are described as if they were physical processes. They are dealt with in terms of molecules, chemical reactions, gradients, concentrations – all terms that are also used in a laboratory. What matters to me in the second level of physiology is the connection with life. Physiological processes care for our life, comprising a system of functions that are attuned to one another and constitute an organically coherent whole. In biology such a system is called an organism. In anthroposophical terminology the word 'body' is also used to indicate this principle. Each one of us has a physical body with a measurable size and weight. Each one of us has a life-body with our own life processes.

The *soul* level and that of our *spirit (self)* are not self-evidently distinguishable for people growing up in the West. In mainstream medicine, psychiatry and healthcare, the term 'soul' is generally considered to refer to our behaviour, despite the fact that behaviour is explained using physical processes that occur in the brain. Are body and soul then the same thing after all? The term 'spirit' is often placed in the realm of religion, and therefore our own individual beliefs.

This not how the classification into four levels is intended. We can simply consult our everyday experience to clarify the distinction between soul and self-spirit. Let's consider the following phrases: I feel great, I fancy a good meal, I control myself. The latter is an interesting expression: I control myself. The self occurs twice in this brief sentence: which self is involved in '*I* control myself' and which in 'I control *myself*'? There is apparently a self that can comment on or influence our behaviour – our soul.

The third level, the level of the soul, includes all the things we experience: our emotions, thoughts, plans – all the conscious and not-so-conscious aspects of our consciousness.

The fourth level, that of self-spirit, relates to the part of us that can distance itself from the contents of our own consciousness, reflect on them and make a judgment about them. Our self-spirit can call our self 'I'. We can consider this level to be unique, a divine spark, our spiritual dimension.

Chapter 2.
How Digital Media Are Changing Us

When people move a lot, or a little, or one-sidedly, their body adapts to it. The muscles, tendons and bones adapt, their metabolism adjusts to its habitual need. The sense of well-being or discomfort that accompanies the pattern of movement becomes familiar, and after a while people no longer notice the change.

This adaptive process of the physical body, the metabolism, the soul and the individual applies to all people at any age. But for children there is another special aspect. In the learning phase of life, approximately until adulthood, adaptations have a tendency to become definitive. Changes literally leave traces on the brain and bones. The general pattern is: the younger the child, the stronger the effect.

Everything we experience has consequences across all four levels of our body and soul. This applies there-fore to our contact with digital media. I will briefly summarise the conseq-uences across the levels of the fourfold human being. However, the consequences always occur simult-aneously across all four levels.

Level 1. Physical consequences

Obesity

Obesity may well be the greatest threat to public health of our times. Our weight is closely related to the chance of cardiovascular diseases, type 2 diabetes and early ageing. For individuals it brings discomfort and illness, and for society enormous costs in healthcare, hence campaigns by Western governments to reduce obesity, as well as and increased interest from health insurers. The most important factors that determine whether adults will become obese are the weight of their parents and their weight as a child. Nutritional habits, of course, play a large role, but the use of digital media also has an impact. Researchers consider various factors to be significant:

- ♠ Spending a lot of time in front of screens often means little movement and therefore little expenditure of energy.

- ♠ Food-related advertisements trick us into feeling hungry and encourage us to eat.

♠ Unhealthy foods are often consumed while watching screens, especially the TV: sugary drinks and rapidly absorbed carbohydrates combined with fat, such as cola and chips.

♠ We use very little energy when we sit passively in front of a screen, even less than when we are resting (see below under basal metabolic rate).

♠ Snacking in front of screens hinders a healthy nutritional pattern. Children no longer have an appetite for the (let's hope) healthy food that's brought to the table.

Eyesight

When children's eyes get accustomed to the flat surface of screens, they find it harder to focus and their eyes adjust less easily. The recent increase in near-sightedness and adjustment disorders of the eyes is probably due to screen use. In the position our eyes take on when looking at a screen[3], they blink less frequently than normal, which causes irritation of the conjunctiva, known as conjunctivitis.[4]

Back problems

Young people who spend a lot of time hunched over games consoles or smartphones are at risk of developing a 'Gameboy back'. This is a serious and sometimes permanent deformity of the upper part of the spine, which can have lifelong consequences in terms of mobility problems and pain. At one time a cervical herniated disc[5] was a rarity. A spinal disc herniation or 'slipped disc' is a common problem developed by people who put undue stress on their spine. It occurs in the lower back, in the hollow above the pelvis. In the case of 'Gameboy back' this hernia also occurs in the hollow near the neck. As with lower-back herniation, nerves can become pinched. Sometimes it's necessary to wear a collar; in other cases surgery is unavoidable. Either way requires a change in posture when sitting and lying down.[6]

Mobility

Gym teachers will confirm that children's flexibility and coordination are decreasing at an alarming rate. Almost all children sit still for hours in front of screens and many children don't participate in a sport. Of course, more factors play a role here. The arrival of schools, and the school desks that came with them, has made children's brains smarter but their backs weaker. It is in fact entirely unnatural for children to sit still for hours on end. Their bodies want to move, play and discover. Although some schools encourage parents to let their children walk to school, most children are brought by car or bus and are dropped off in front of the school gates then picked up again. As everyone knows: watching screens requires virtually no movement. Every hour in front of a screen means an hour less for developing mobility.

The brain

We know from brain physiology that everything we do (acting, feeling, thinking) leaves a trace on the brain. The path used for an action, feeling or thought, the connections that are used and the network in which it happens remain open. When the same path is used again, it's easier than the first time. You probably recognise this: when practising a piece of music it's easy to repeat the mistake we made the first time; after finding the route to a certain address for the first time, the second time we're inclined to take the same route again; in mathematics, long division can be done in various ways, but the way we first learned it is logged in our system; when we first met a certain person we immediately thought 'what a good-looking man' (or 'what a stuck-up fool') and now we can't shake off that first impression.

Therefore we know that if such a path is followed not once but often, it anchors itself not only functionally but also physically: in the soul, but also in the brain. Everything we do regularly determines the structure of our brain. Here the following rule also applies: the younger the child, the greater the tendency for habitual paths to determine physical structure. This structure in turn then comes to determine our actions, feelings and thoughts, facilitated by the earlier events that occasioned the physical structure in the brain. We might say that those events are imaged in the brain.

From this point on, people who think that our

behaviour is determined by our brain are right – at least in part, for the structures in the brain have a measure of fixedness, but they are not unchangeable. New habits of acting, feeling and thinking modify the brain. All adults can steadily and effectively educate their brain, though more slowly than when they were children. This is called plasticity.

In addition, a certain capacity to generalise occurs. People who learn to observe acutely with their sense of hearing, musicians for example, can mobilise this capability outside of their profession. Such people 'hear', in the metaphorical sense of the word, what resonates in a conversation, what lies behind the words. They have a capacity for noticing the rhythm, the timbre, the dissonances in a conversation. Another example: someone who has learned through mathematics to think in exact terms can apply this capacity to thinking exactly in other areas of life. We therefore benefit more generally from learning all kinds of different skills. We may never need the specific skill again, but the pattern that has formed in both our habits and brain frequently comes in useful later, often in unexpected ways.

This, incidentally, is an important justification for the school curriculum. Although children will never need to use the majority of what we teach them in later life, the capacity that has been created within their brains will serve them well.

Let's return to the effect of digital media and screens on children's brains. Which capacities do children acquire through viewing them and what physical structures are established in the brain? Little is known about the long-term effects of the frequent use of screens. Obviously much depends on environmental factors, such as the extent of use, compensating activities, temperament and so on. These factors make it difficult to measure the precise impact, which is exacerbated because researchers carrying out the study in thirty years, time will be constituted differently from the people asking the question today.

Level 2. Life processes

Everything we do has consequences for our physiology, our life processes. Therefore when children spend a lot of time using digital media we can expect to see physiological consequences. These consequences are not positive. Screen time is not vitalising and it does not make us healthy. It has a strong tendency to disturb biorhythms, it devours energy and time, it is exhausting. These factors can be serious, especially when they are not compensated for by energy-giving activities that make us fit. Surely digital media isn't unique in these negative effects? No, it's not unique. It's a general phenomenon that we get tired over the course of the day and our energy dwindles. It's the necessary effect of consciousness. We 'buy' an alert consciousness with degradation of our vitality. This is why healthy people alternate activities that require mental alertness with activities that recharge. This is why we need sleep. The topic of this book requires two short comments on the phenomenon of fatigue.

FATIGUE: SATISFIED AND EXHAUSTED

We can feel tired and satisfied after performing an intellectual task, such as playing a chess match. We can also feel tired and wrung out after performing a task that requires conscious focus. Consider for yourself which kind of activity results in one or the other kind of fatigue. It's comparable with physical exertion. Everyone can understand feeling tired-and-satisfied as well as tired-and-exhausted. In the first case we rapidly recover and in the end our fatigue makes us stronger. In the second case recovery takes longer and yields less.

FATIGUE: QUALITY OF SLEEP

Why do we sometimes wake up in the morning feeling rested and full of energy and at other times weary and stiff? Of course, it depends on environmental conditions such as how comfortable our bed is and whether mosquitoes were bothering us – in other words, how the night in fact went. But the main factor in determining quality of sleep is how we spent the hours before falling asleep. It varies for different people, but everyone has experienced occasions when anxieties, alcohol, a heavy meal or an unpleasant conversation have undermined the revitalising quality of sleep. Whereas a good conversation, a pleasant encounter or a beautiful concert can all enhance sleep. It's therefore important to ask, if we're watching a screen before bedtime, in which of these two categories does the media we're consuming fall?

Day-night rhythm

The invention of artificial light has given people in the developed world the freedom to ignore day and night as determinants of waking and sleeping. Screens lengthen the day even further, and not just because the off-switch on a TV or computer is even more difficult to find than an old-fashioned light switch. An engrossing book or an interesting visit can extend the day past midnight, but there is an interesting and essential difference. When we read a book or have a conversation we have to keep our attention focused, which is barely necessary when it comes to screens. Screens work themselves deep into the life processes of our brains, into our biology. The production of the sleep hormone melatonin is suppressed, the production of the happiness hormone dopamine and of the alertness hormone serotonin is stimulated. In front of screens our (and our children's) brains work differently: they are artificially changed to waking brains. You may see parallels here with the effect of drugs, which is correct – screens function in the same way. The stimulating work of screens happens quickly, after a mere few seconds – even with a small smartphone screen.

Children with a TV or computer in their room are at a much greater risk of sleep disturbance. Experts have issued serious warnings: allowing children to have a TV in their room is negligent. Although these experts were right, reality has caught up with them. Many school-age children now have a TV or computer in their room. This is handy because each member of the family can watch their own TV programme. But it's also a serious concern because lack of sleep is an important factor in developing learning problems, lack of concentration, behavioural problems such as ADHD, and disturbances in the body's immune system.

Digestion rhythms

Shared family meals are less common these days. This is often due to longer working hours, as well as the use of microwaves, which allow family members to warm up their own meal when required. Another factor (from a nutritional perspective, a bad habit) is eating in front of screens. Paying attention to our food is essential for digestion: food that has been observed can be more easily digested; food that is hastily ingested encounters an unprepared gastrointestinal tract. Distracting children when they're eating at the table is itself a concern. Shovelling in food in front of the TV while children are in a disconnected mode guarantees digestive disturbances.

A second principle for maintaining a healthy functioning digestive system is the sensation of having an empty stomach. Rhythm is the carrier wave of life. When applied to digestion, this means having regular eating times, when we're feeling hungry. In general this means three main meals with three snacks in between and nothing else. Eating rhythm is comparable for our digestive tract to breathing in and out for the lungs, and to sleeping and waking for the human being as a whole. What does this have to do with digital media, you may ask? In front of screens children like to snack and graze, consuming sugary drinks and foods like potato chips, which is one reason why obesity is strongly related to screen time.

Is our digestion really that important? Yes, this is serious. The digestive system is at least as important as a good brain for healthy functioning because it must tolerate, process and incorporate everything we consume. A well-educated digestive and ingestive system provides the basis for a strong immune system and good health.

Basal metabolic rate

The metabolism of a person at rest is called the basal metabolic rate. As soon as we do something, whether it's reading a book, conversing, walking or running, our metabolic rate increases. A surprising finding is that the metabolic rate of someone sitting in front of the TV decreases relative to the basal metabolic rate. We might assume watching TV is still 'doing something', but from a metabolic perspective, this is not the case. When we're watching TV our energy conversion becomes less than basal, lower than when we sleep. Any snacks we consume when watching TV are therefore metabolised more slowly than when we are at rest, making an extra contribution to weight gain.

Memory and learning

Now I want to discuss why memory and learning involve not only cognitive functions but life functions: health, resistance and recuperative capacity. Children set out to learn and remember things using exactly the same powers used to grow and stay healthy. Rudolf Steiner [1] made this discovery at the beginning of the twentieth century. It may well be his most significant discovery.

Steiner had thoroughly studied Goethe's[7] scientific work and held it in high esteem. Goethe discovered that all parts of a plant can be reduced to one starting point: the leaf on the stem. By means of systematic transformations (which he called metamorphoses) not only can the successive leaf shapes be formed, but also the flower petals, stamen, stigma, fruit and seeds. The same building material leads, via the principle of metamorphosis, to very different phenomena. This principle of metamorphosis, Steiner discovered, also applies to life forces in people, which can be best studied by observing children as they grow up. If we have an eye for it we can see it, and if we don't have an eye for it we can learn to see it. The building principles of growth, resistance and recuperative capacity are also used for learning and for memory.

For example, children's growth involves an increase in the number of cells – but not only that. The cells fit into a totality, namely that of the whole child, but the whole is not fixed because the child is always growing. Exactly the same applies to children's learning capacity. All new knowledge fits into the life experience children have already acquired up to that point (their memory), but this life experience doesn't remain the same because it grows. It nevertheless remains a unity, closely connected with that particular child and with what that child experiences.

This, incidentally, is a more specific example of what was said before about the polarity of consciousness and vitality (see sections on Fatigue, p.31). When the use of digital media has a negative effect on children's memory and their capacity for learning, we may surmise that it also therefore affects their biology. But even without Steiner's discovery, people can work out the link between learning, memory and vitality for themselves. Have you ever tried to learn something new or remember something in particular after a sleepless night – the name of a new colleague, the book a friend recommended, what your children are supposed to take to school tomorrow? After a period of illness, even just a bad cold, our memory functions less well than usual for a few days. After delivering a baby, women are often not clear-headed, certainly if they are sharing their vitality through breastfeeding.

Perhaps the best proof for the connection between learning and vitality is sleep. How often do we find that a problem has resolved itself spontaneously by the next morning? The Dutch word for solved (*opgelost*) also means dissolved: the problem has been taken up into the greater whole, and the answer finds us.

Are we getting smarter?

It is indeed as we might expect: outsourcing memory to an external storage device is a disaster for our internal memory. The invention of printing was the first great blow (see p.16), and with the advent of virtually unlimited digital storage capacity the human memory has become more or less superfluous. As students say: why should I remember it when I can simply look it up? The great difference is, of course, that what I remember myself belongs to me, has become part of myself, of my conscious self and my unconscious self. What I have stored in an external memory drive has not become part of myself. Or should I formulate it the other way around? Have I perhaps outsourced part of myself to a machine? It may sound strange, but this is not so far from the truth. Viewed from the broader human perspective we can determine that our collective memory, the collective subconscious, has been shifted in part to the storage computers of Google and suchlike. For individual people, for ourselves and our children, it may still look a bit different.

On the basis of our life experience and aptitude we

are perhaps blessed with a healthy memory, but great numbers of people will come to suffer from memory loss. The more we use digital media, the greater our memory loss may be. This is one of the messages expressed by Manfred Spitzer in his book, *Digitale Demenz* (Digital dementia).[8] But there is another quite different perspective, which is, for example, eloquently expressed in the book, *Smarter Than You Think: How Technology Is Changing Our Minds for the Better* by Clive Thompson.[9] Groups of young people solve, for example, shared problems they encounter in new video games. While the makers hope they've made the game so complex that it will last two years into the future, a group of teenagers may solve it in two weeks – via forums that exist for this purpose or have been started by themselves, sometimes internationally. This is indeed a striking use of shared knowledge and communal smartness.

Nor is Thompson all that afraid of memory loss. He talked with a number of people who have spent years tracking their entire lives with webcams and microphones, and who have continual access to large databases. They have quite literally stored their lives in an external memory – much more complete than human memory, which is often unreliable. The people Thompson interviewed were satisfied, and considered the possibility of consulting an exact, accurate memory an advantage. In the conversation, the subjects came across, according to the author, as quite normal and social. Thompson does mention a limitation of the system: deciding whether and what to consult in our external memory still relies on a human being with imperfections. This problem could be solved if computer software is developed to remind us of important things, such as regular tasks we need to fulfil.

The opening chapters of *Smarter Than You Think* are devoted to artificial intelligence, as illustrated by the chess computer that defeated chess grandmaster Kasparov. Kasparov was not overly surprised and took control of the situation by collaborating with the chess computer, which turned out to be a good move. The combination of human intuition and the brute calculation power of the computer appeared to be unbeatable, and superior to the two parties individually. We might say that chess is very complex but also very exact mathematically. It's logical that a computer would be very good at it. But could a computer deal with common questions from real life? At the end of the book Thompson describes his competition with a know-it-all computer, which has an enormous number of reference tools about all possible subjects. You guessed it: the human being lost, and not by a narrow margin.

Patti Valkenburg, a professor of media, youth and society at the University of Amsterdam, takes an intermediary position.[10] On the basis of the available scientific literature she describes how difficult it is as a scholar to gain a sound opinion concerning the influence of digital media on child development. She warns against strong statements, since a scientific argument can generally be found to back up several viewpoints. The rapid growth and development in this area mean investigations into effects lag behind reality. Her conclusions and recommendations are therefore so nuanced and general that they do not provide us with much to go on.

The Arab Spring has made many people enthusiastic about the revolutionary possibilities of social media such as Facebook and Twitter. Within a few days or weeks social media made it possible to mobilise great masses of people to take to the streets and demonstrate. Furthermore, they enabled relief measures for wounded demonstrators to be coordinated efficiently and effectively. Relief supplies were acquired and directed to the right place by means of social networks and much was achieved by small organisations. Unfortunately, the so-called Islamic State extremists have has shown that social media can also be used very effectively for amoral purposes. They sow fear and entice followers in a modern and appealing way.

   The use of digital media, including social media, thus makes deep inroads into human life, including people's life functions.

Level 3. The soul: thinking, feeling, the will

What, actually, is the soul? For me the soul is the stage upon which our experiences unfold. Hate and love, despair and hope, foolishness and insight do not have any power as abstractions. They are only significant when they become experiences in the human soul; sensations and feelings, opinions and intentions become reality through people. It is therefore hugely important *which* sensations, feelings, opinions and intentions we give access to our soul. We let them, as it were, perform as characters on the stage of our inner world. Our nervous system plays a role in this, but not an active one. The nervous system enables us to be conscious of our sensations, feelings, opinions and intentions. The stage manager, namely we ourselves, can invite or exclude certain characters, and this stage-manager role forms the basis of raising children.

Circumstances may seriously limit the stage manager's freedom of action. When we're hungry we are preoccupied with bodily sensations and processes – hunger and eating – and our thoughts and feelings are restricted. Fear, despair, loneliness, worry, stress and depression can dominate in a comparable manner, playing the lead role on the stage of the soul.

Something similar happens in addiction. We can get addicted to anything: alcohol, other stimulants, eating, sex, violence, money, power, status and so on.

The characteristic of addiction is how difficult it is to kick the habit, to free up the stage for other characters. As if drawn by an invisible force the familiar actors re-enter the stage and begin to play their dominant role again. This invisible force becomes visible or at least noticeable when withdrawal symptoms make their appearance: fear, panic, headaches, sweating, throwing up, diarrhoea, fever, low temperature. Then it becomes apparent how deeply the addiction has lodged itself in the soul and body. Many people cannot deal with 'going cold turkey'. In drug rehabilitation centres these people are given chemical substances to make the process more bearable.

Logically parents should only allow children access to activities such as working on the computer, gaming and watching TV when there is no chance of those activities taking over the dominant role onstage in our children's souls – or so we might think. 'Computer and TV in the raising of children is a worldwide experiment with an unpredictable result and without a control group.' This statement was made in 2003.[11] Since then we have already learned a lot about the result: excess use of digital media correlates with feelings of loneliness and stress, social isolation, aggressiveness, agitation and ADHD behaviour, lack of imagination, learning difficulties, and becoming the victim of bullying.

Level 4. We ourselves, the self

You may be wondering: Is no realm within us safe from the influence of digital media? I must disappoint you: the answer is no. But that in itself doesn't tell us anything about the media as such. It doesn't tell us anything about the influence of everything a child experiences growing up. This influence plays by definition on all four levels of the human being discussed in this chapter. In the previous section we introduced the self as stage manager – never on the stage, but standing in the wings. During the performance the stage manager sits among the audience with the spectators and gains the role of conscience. In this role our self observes our experiences from outside. Is the self then always hidden? Does it stay tucked away in the wings or in the anonymity of the audience? Does it never appear onstage?

Everything that takes place in the world can manifest itself on the stage of the soul, including the self. When children begin to call themselves 'I', at about two-and-a-half years old, they take the stage very briefly. All children know they're unique because they only call themself 'I'. This is presented brilliantly in a small book by Willem van der Does and Peter van Straaten[12] in which the types of people described and illustrated show what we become without a sense of self – a mere stereotype or character. Viewed from the perspective of the self we are human beings, spiritual beings on earth, with the potential qualities for becoming a stage manager. Over the course of our childhood this stage manager, if all is well, will make an appearance step by step. We take the first step by saying 'I'. From that time on children know they have a self. The second step is taken halfway through high school when children become aware that their individual self is different from that of all other human beings. The third step comes at the end of puberty when young people start to take responsibility for themselves.

Several important aids support children as they take these steps. To begin with, speech enables children to name what they experience. Language development is the basis for many developmental steps. It is a precondition of children naming their 'self', and it makes the self a reality to children! Speaking apparently has a magical effect: it makes things real.

The second aid is play. Children get to know themselves and the world around them by exploring reality through play. They discover that we can change things and control them. Imagination is the force that enables them to explore. People wouldn't get very far without imagination, fantasy and play. Often in adult life our creative imagination (creativity) enables us to manage life.

The third aid is restraint. If in the restless stream of life there are no moments of restraint, becoming ourselves is bound to fail. What do we really want? Who are we really? What is the purpose of all of this? These are questions for adolescents. Questions that can only find an answer in moments of rest, inner silence and restraint. Intense activity can bring many achievements and it can be addictive, but being able to step back, stand still and reflect are typically human skills; without them we can't become ourselves. Parents can encourage this in their children – not so much by asking them what they want to be when they grow up, or by presenting them with moral choices, but by appreciating the fact that a toddler may be naughty and a schoolchild may get bored. Being naughty means stepping out of everyday life – most often not in order to harass Mum, but to see whether it can be done, whether we can succeed at stepping out of the stream of expectations. Being bored is similar: every healthy child has an abundance of ideas for playing and planning; every healthy child occasionally steps back from activity and gets bored. 'Mom, I'm bored' – 'That's OK, dear'.

What about digital media and these aids for the development of the self? Screens are no help in the acquisition of language. Considerable screen use, in particular watching so-called language acquisition programmes, delays language development. This is logical: children learn to speak from other people. Screens are no help in learning restraint. On the contrary, they are a kind of anti-boredom machine. Video games are based on quick rewards and reflex behaviour: players must react without reflection like a machine, not like a human being.

Some games are based on collaboration, an important factor in raising children. However collaboration, when looked at closely, mostly depends on a well understood self-interest. If you do this for me, I'll do that for you... There's nothing wrong with it, but it doesn't contribute towards the development of a free, autonomous, conscientious human being. Many games and films present a profusion of nudity, violence and drama. Human solidarity, patience and restraint are not mediagenic, and least of all boredom.

So what can we conclude about the consequences of using digital media? It would seem they bring about considerable misery and harm. This is not the fault of the various forms of media or electronic devices themselves, but of the people who unwittingly, and let's assume with good intentions, allow their children so much access to them. 'Technology is neither good nor bad; nor is it neutral'.[13]

The wide-ranging effects across the levels of the fourfold human being can, certainly for children, be called reasonably disastrous. If this book were to end here, it would be a sad story, but it does not...

Chapter 3.
Underlying Interests of the Digital World

In Chapters 1 and 2 I highlighted the scale of digital media's impact on people, individual children and the earth, and revealed many negative effects. This concern not only applies to digital media: prosperity in the West has been achieved without full awareness of the consequences for the earth and its inhabitants. Resource depletion, problems with waste products, including radioactive waste, global warming and rising sea levels are examples of our negative impact on the planet. The extreme and continually growing gap between rich and poor, profits from the sales of weapons and drugs, the increasing violence against existing or invented minorities are all consequences of our 'progress'. The individual suffering many people experience from diseases brought on by luxury and by poverty – hunger, AIDS, the Ebola virus, resistance to antibiotics – is rarely the result of individuals' own choices; rather, they are related to 'the ways of our world'.

In the case of the weapons industry and the drug trade it's fairly clear where the underlying interests lie: in individual enrichment and the exercise of power. It's disconcerting that these interests override the well-being of other individuals, societies, nations and the earth. Every right-minded person knows that there are questionable aspects to the weapons and drug trades.

But it's not so simple, I believe, to identify the interests that have made digital media so powerful and dominant. They have acquired the sheen of renewal and progress. Modernisation in education and healthcare means without exception the expansion of information and communications technology – against our better judgment, as many critics have told us.[14] No one can reasonably maintain that we haven't been warned.

Money

First let's discuss the role of money. Large companies such as Apple, Microsoft and Google are not charitable institutions. They hitchhike on the wave of optimism that washes ashore on all the world's beaches called 'progress-thanks-to-technology'. Are the CEOs of Apple, Microsoft and Google then the main culprits? Are they the money-hungry chief scoundrels who make the world deliberately dependent on modern technology? I would say: of course not. But when focused on profit, most people think less about the well-being of others, and this includes the directors of large companies.

Besides, isn't money always a manifestation of something else? 'Money is the lifeblood of the economy': look for the money streams to find what society wants, just as our blood is the carrier of our will. When we're happy to pay more for something sustainable, isn't that an expression of our will? When we invest millions in fireworks on New Year's Eve, isn't that an expression of our collective will? Or do we merely do it out of habit? That's possible, which makes us realise that habits are closely related to will, like the will without consciousness. They have carved a channel and become a matter of course.

Our conclusion has to be that money and will are closely related. With this in mind let's take another look at the mega-sums that circulate in the innovation, marketing and trade of electronic devices.

Will

The two main motivations behind the money streams we're talking about here are *power* and *diversion*. More bluntly we can call them *aggression* and *sex*, or *contempt for people* and *the glorification of people*. The following is derived from anthroposophy. Anthroposophy did not invent these two forces, but the way Rudolf Steiner described them helps us to recognise them. And that is necessary because recognition is an important aid in protecting ourselves against their influence.

Like everything that occurs in the world, our two motivating forces, *power* and *diversion,* can appear as characters on the stage of the human soul. They are influential characters, which appear in every theatrical or operatic performance. In Gounod's *Faust*[15], for example, Mephistopheles appears in a variety of guises. Some clearly have the signature of *power*, others of *diversion*.

In all the cultural output of digital media we can easily recognise both of these two operative forces. That is no different from any other cultural medium, such as drama, music or dance, but we can also see these forces at work in educational innovations and banking crises, the inventions of printing and electricity, as well as in social movements such as the Enlightenment and Romanticism.

Viewed in this way there is no movement, influence or aspect of culture in which these two characters do not play a significant role. They are therefore quite common, almost commonplace. Yet they do not deserve a following. They are one-sided and lead people away from being human. When craving *power* people become fearful dictators, when craving *diversion* people become irresponsible libertines.

What we must do is find the 'golden mean', a happy medium. This is not a colourless compromise or a dull grey between black and white. The golden mean is valuable, colourful, like the red morning and evening sky. Goethe would use the concept of *Steigerung* here: the polarities (light and darkness) resolve themselves and let something new appear (the colours), of a higher order.[16]

It is time for an example. In the start-up phase of an organisation, fervour, originality, imagination and innovation dominate. *Diversion* helps to make working together pleasant and light-hearted. After a few years, the workers begin to get annoyed with improvisation and lack of structure. Rules are drawn up that everyone must follow. At first this is done playfully, but soon the need arises for more clarity. Sanctions are imposed on breaking the rules. When *power* gets its way, a layer of management is installed that has the final say. This in turn brings further dissatisfaction. Now comes a crucial phase in the organisation's development. Will it be possible to choose neither the conviviality of the past nor for the rigid structures of the present, but something new? Can the workers jointly come to a structure that fits this specific organisation? Elements such as taking care of one another, feeling appreciated, feeling that everyone is involved in something valuable, earning money – all these must find a place in the new organisation. If they succeed, the organisation can continue to grow successfully.

The role of Power

So let's return to the topic of this chapter: the interests that let digital media gain ground.

The power of electronic media is manifest: screens keep children in their power with invisible chains. The attraction of any moving image on a screen is enormous. Even a hyperactive child will sit quietly in front of a screen. The power screens exercise, which can lead to addiction, moves among other things via substances in the brain (neurotransmitters), which give us a thrill and make us feel good. Once addicted we really are in their power.

The contents of the programme also exercise power. Advertising has considerable power over children, which is why it's such a booming industry. Any supermarket that doesn't stock the candy, chocolate spread, toys and stickers that are advertised inexorably loses out, and if we want to stay on good terms with our kids, it's easier not to shop there.

Power and violence are over-represented in TV programmes and certainly in video games for young people. This begins with shooting down extraterrestrials from space and ends with realistic, horrible bloodbaths among virtual humans. The number of deaths the average eighteen-year-old has seen on screen runs into the tens of thousands, as does the number of on-screen deaths they have caused themselves. Of course, not all programmes and video games are violent, but those that aren't are often less fun to play. And besides, the power exerted by the *Teletubbies*, for example, is not so coarse, but it is still enormous. Small children imitate everything, including the silly little cries of the silly humanoids on screen.

An effective way to exercise control is to let everything happen quickly. The on-screen images don't allow enough time for the human soul to digest them. In real life, after receiving a new impression or stimulus there is a pause in our attention for a fraction of a second, which provides physiological protection against over-stimulation.[17] In front of the screen this protection falls away and images pour themselves unhindered into defenceless children. It's logical, therefore, that children become over-stimulated and feel out of sorts. After all, detachment, observing from a distance, is one of the conditions for the functioning of the self.

A NOTE ON EFFICIENCY

Speed and efficiency are connected. Many high-tech gadgets are marketed using the word 'efficient'. What does this mean? In most cases it means that what we had to do ourselves in the past can now be done by a machine. Handy! The same work is done by fewer people in less time and therefore costs less money. Is that really an advantage? It has, in any case, some significant disadvantages. It costs jobs – too bad for the people who had work but now sit at home; too bad for the loss of their valuable experience. Those now unemployed had the capacity and experience to foresee situations and solve them on the shop floor; machines do not gain such well-rounded experience and cannot interact creatively with unexpected situations.

In the past I did the administration of my pediatric practice on cards, later in paper files. I wrote invoices myself once a month, later I typed them. There were hardly any payment problems. Now I send my bills using the binary number system to a firm that turns them into invoices. The result is: lots of payment problems, lots of errors that must be traced and corrected in a time-consuming process. Each year we get new rules to which the accounts are subject. I estimate that it costs me twice as much time to deal with my financial administration. What do you mean: efficient?

A beauty parlour in our town had ordered one sample of a product. A few days later eleven large boxes were delivered with 1111 samples. A finger had stayed just a bit too long on the 1-key. Mistakes are made, human error happens now and then.

But wasn't the sales pitch about efficiency? This often isn't the case. 'Can you attend our meeting at 11 am on Monday?' 'No, but I can be there next Monday at 11.' 'Sorry, we're busy then.' 'Could you do 9 am?' 'Yes, I have to rearrange something but I can be there'. 'OK, agreed.' This conversation in person or over the telephone takes one minute. But for 'efficiency' reasons the business where my wife works has introduced the rule that all correspondence goes via email. The result: five emails spread over eight days. Time taken: fifteen minutes.

The electronic delivery of data invites us to collect more and more data. Hospitals must deliver their quality parameters, schools their educational results, physicians the data from their practice. More and more each year. Efficient? Certainly not, because each inspection, municipality or health-insurance company has its own format in which the data must be delivered.

The role of Diversion

Diversion is also an integral part of the digital media phenomenon, for example, in the form of entertainment. For children television has made learning fun. We can be entertained all evening (and night, and day). After a long, busy day we let ourselves slump onto the couch in front of the screen to relax and divert our thoughts. Deep down we know beforehand that after a few hours we'll go to bed grouchy because we could have done something better with our time, the programme probably won't be very good and we probably won't really get to relax. And when we go to bed in bad spirits, we may not sleep well.

Digital media also encourage us to switch rapidly between one activity and another – a form of attention deficit. Multitasking doesn't really exist: it's an attention deficit problem.[18] An individual can do one thing with full attention. When we do two or more things at the same time, we do all of them less effectively. Some adolescents can do it, and an adolescent with ADHD has the advantage here.

Sex is equally as over-represented on screen as violence: sex as diversion, watching how others do it. It's now even difficult for children to get through primary school without being confronted, intentionally or unintentionally, with sex on screen, which is damaging. Experts then say: let's provide sex education earlier. In The Netherlands, the Foundation for Non-commercial Advertising (SIRE, *Stichting Ideëele Reclame*) ran a campaign with the title, 'Talk to your child about sex before the internet does'. Watching TV brings earlier sexual development, even without viewing adult-only films. The term 'Generation XXX' has been used to describe the current generation of children who grow up with pornography as a diversion and means of finding out about sex.

Of course, there are also good programmes on TV: films, nature documentaries, concerts, shows and interviews. But if I honestly ask myself which programmes I really don't want to miss, very few remain, but this may be different for you.

The combination of Power and diversion

What is exceptional with regard to digital media is, in my opinion, that *power* and *diversion* work together more than ever before. Power provides the exciting new technology – the *screen*, we might say. Diversion creates the distraction, the detachment, the high – the *image*, we might say.[19]

This may be the right moment to address those who suspect I've fallen victim to a conspiracy theory: an invisible evil force that intends to harm humans and cunningly take control of the earth. No, I don't believe in a conspiracy theory, but yes, the earth and its inhabitants are in danger. Instead of talking about a conspiracy I would say: we do not need a conspiracy to explain the degrading abuses in the world. People do this to each other. The fact that tablets, which have been proven to have a negative impact on child development, are being introduced in nursery classes, is not the result of a conspiracy; it is done with good intentions.

No human actions are alien to us. *Power* and *diversion* appear on the stage of everyone's soul. It helps to recognise them in all kinds of phenomena in society and to give them a name. Then we can view them as important characters on the stage of our soul and choose not to identify with them.

So to answer the question: Which interests are the driving force behind the proliferation of digital media? The preliminary answer is: the common human interests we recognise under the names *power* and *diversion*.

Can we not say anything more positive about the interests we've identified? Am I suffering from a contemporary form of historical chauvinism – people's tendency to consider the time in which they live to be excessively important? I view it a little differently, as I will explain below.

The positive aspects are at least as voluminous as the book by Clive Thompson, *Smarter than You Think*, which I mentioned before (see p.38). The gains in our communication systems, for example in connection with our safety, are obvious. The ease with which we can quickly look up information is wonderful. But that is not where the crux lies.

Of course, each era considers itself important. It would be strange to hear someone say, 'We live in such dull and insignificant times. Take the eighteenth century, the era of the Enlightenment, I wish I could have lived back then.' In every era people have to choose their own viewpoints in the midst of the challenges of that specific period. The motivation for doing so is called development. Children have no choice but to develop. Adults usually choose to move themselves and the world forward, to develop. Each generation in each era has a new task in this race forward.

The course of development that comes about in each era relates to the inventions of that time. During the Industrial Revolution the invention of machines had a huge impact and brought about changes in control and power. In the sixties, the era of 'flower power', we saw a desire to break free from the establishment, let go of old values, focus more on diversion. We can look back on earlier time periods and ask the question: did it turn out well? Were the developments positive? What was achieved and what were the side effects?

In order to answer those questions we will have to choose a yardstick to measure the developments against. Let's choose the concept of 'humanity' – or human dignity and solidarity (see 'Being ourselves', p.71). The development of culture proceeds in phases. In the course of development we are more or less focused on ourselves or on the community. The trust in external powers such as religion and science alternates. A cultural shift takes place when a society becomes too one-sided. Human dignity and solidarity bring us back to the middle ground and keep society on track: they are yardsticks against which we can determine whether the developments of the digital era fall within, below or above acceptable standards.[20]

Chapter 4.
How Digital Media Are Changing Parenting

The Dutch publication *Iene Miene Media* annually polls a representative group of parents on their opinions about media use by young children up to the age of seven.[21] It appears most parents happily allow their children to use digital media, and listed the following positive considerations:

- Children can learn by means of digital media in an enjoyable way.

- Communication via Skype – for example, with a father in a foreign country or a friend who has moved away.

- Learning to share the device.

- Learning to focus attention.

- Keeping up with their peers.

♠ Good for general development and learning the English language.

But they also have genuine concerns, and list the following negative considerations:

♠ Less time for playing outside, which parents consider to be more important.

♠ Left to themselves, unmonitored, kids can go further than intended and explore unsuitable content.

♠ Kids no longer play and are no longer creative.

♠ The risk of online grooming.

♠ Parents are uncertain about the suitability of some programmes, games and apps.

Most parents don't find it difficult to make their own rules for regulating their children's screen time, but feel it can be a difficult subject to broach with the parents of their children's friends; it seems many parents don't switch on the parental control functions of their devices and they don't monitor their children's activity afterwards. Three quarters of parents monitor their children's screen time, but one quarter does not. About two thirds of parents have no problem telling their children when to stop using devices, but one third does.

In May 2014 the journal *Medisch Contact* (Medical Contact) examined the topic of digital media,[22] describing a number of consequences of screen use from a medical perspective. They noted problems such as a decreasing function of the motor system, lack of sleep, problems with eyes and vision, and internet addiction. This article, in contrast to the findings of *Iene Miene Media*, focused on parents' uncertainty. They recommended that a comprehensive plan for media education must be established to flag the dangers of digital media and educate those involved in raising children. In the list of recommendations to parents, the authors of the article seemed quite ahead of customary practice. They suggested:

- Limiting total screen time to less than two hours per day outside of school.

- Preferably no screen time for children under the age of two.

- No TVs or smartphones in children's bedrooms.

- No screen time during the hour before bedtime.

- Being aware of and discussing the content children view on the internet.

- Establishing media rules for the household.

- Taking a critical look at our own use of digital media.

Are these recommendations merely old-fashioned? Physicians in general seem to be very keen on technical and electronic devices. Are they applying a double standard: one for themselves and one for their clients? (During a doctor's appointment, have you ever noticed that doctors sometimes seem more interested in the screen than in you?)

When I tried to survey the area covered in this chapter, I was struck by the fact that parents have asked very few questions about the effects screen time has on children. We as parents have all found ourselves, as a matter of course, perhaps even eagerly, in a climate where screens are playing a leading role in our children's lives. It strikes me that we have been extremely naive when it comes to media innovations. Why do we let children make a purchase via the internet, at our expense, before we prevent it from happening again? How did we allow online bullying to reach such drastic proportions before noticing and taking action to prevent it? I call this the stair-gate problem. Do we let children fall down the stairs before we decide to install a stair gate? No: we take preventative measures.

Why have serious problems resulting from the use of screens occurred before we've decided to take preventative measures? I feel that we've collectively landed in this realm of new innovation, and only after the fact are we being gradually confronted with the consequences. Furthermore, there is, as yet, no helpline to call for advice.

What is the actual situation? Children spend a lot of time using tablets and are often online from a very young age. Each year this is extending to more hours at an even younger age. It's easy to outsource the acquisition of learning to a tablet: topics like how the world works, how to play, how to behave socially, what's beautiful and what's ugly, what constitutes amusing behaviour and unpleasant behaviour, how to deal with setbacks, with violence and with sexuality. Online they are 'offline' with regard to their parents' efforts at parenting, but they are absorbing external influences of... indeed, of what? The more hours our children spend online, the less we are involved as parents. While this makes some parents feel insecure and powerless, most of them (about three quarters) do not feel that way at all. How can this be? I've found a few explanations. Maybe you recognise some of these:

- We can't prevent it, so it's better to go along with it and enjoy it.

- If it's harmful, 'they' would have done something about it.

- I enjoy using digital media, so why wouldn't I let my children enjoy it too?

- If I don't go along I'll be considered old-fashioned, and that's the last thing I want to be.

- There truly are more important things in the world to worry about than the influence of digital media.

Screens have thoroughly changed parenting over the past decade. All parents must share their role as educator with 'educators' from all over the world who are in touch with their children in the digital sphere. A quarter of parents of young children declare that they do not (or cannot) supervise screen time and digital activity. And from puberty most parents no longer have any idea what their children are getting up to online; it's impossible to find out, since a lot of digital activity takes place outside the home, via smartphones.

Is it perhaps indeed indigenous to our era that children are raised by influences from all around the world? Does this make them 'global citizens'? I don't think so – rather the opposite. Young children must first get to know their own very small world before they can tolerate the learning that comes from the vast wider world.

Alongside this, a very interesting countermovement is taking place. While our children have more freedom to find content and information from anywhere in the world, their freedom to physically roam is decreasing. A Dutch daily newspaper recently published an article entitled 'Big mother is watching you' about apps parents can use to monitor the whereabouts of their children.[23] The article cites the book *Paranoic Parenting* by the British sociologist Frank Furedi.[24] Modern society wants to eliminate all risks, but the price we pay is less room for children to experiment. Has society become less safe? Not so. Traffic accidents and other physical injuries have decreased. The British organisation *Natural England* published research that showed on the basis of a map how children over four generations have lost the 'right to roam'.[25] In 1919 when he was a young boy, great-grandfather George was allowed to go fishing 6 miles (10 km) from home. Grandfather Jack was allowed to go only 1 mile (1.5 km) from home. Mother Vicky was permitted to go by herself to the swimming pool, 1/2 mile (800 m) from home. In 2007 son Ed was allowed go to the end of the street, 300 yards (300 m). Yet risk in the digital world doesn't seem to register at all. Perhaps it's not only physicians who have double standards? We seem to have one standard for everyday life and another for screen life...

An Interlude on Child Development: Becoming Ourselves, Being Ourselves

Becoming ourselves

In the period during which children are in our care, they go through three major phases:

- ♠ Becoming human beings
- ♠ Becoming fellow human beings
- ♠ Becoming themselves

If children could put into words what they require from their upbringing, they might say, 'Help us to become ourselves as human beings.' From the perspective of developmental physiology it is of the utmost importance that children first receive the opportunity to learn general human skills, then to become members of the group to which they belong, and only then to discover who they themselves actually are.

This is true of all children: of the millions of modern

children who come into this world awake and clear-headed, who at eighteen months call themselves 'I' and at three start running the household; and of the thousands of children who find their way through slower development and learning difficulties. We cannot give precise age periods for the three phases because they overlap, and especially because they are experienced several times, each time in the same sequence. Here are a few examples:

1. In their first year, children learn to stand and walk, in their second year to listen and speak, and in their third year to observe and think. Standing and walking is done by all able-bodied people in the world, listening and speaking connects children with their linguistic companions, and through observing and having their own thoughts children teach themselves to think.

2. In the pre-school period, when young children are at home or in kindergarten, they get to know general human needs and skills, such as eating and drinking, occupying space and making room for others, and learning to use the toilet. In the primary school period they learn the needs and skills required to belong to a shared culture, a group. They learn to read, write and do arithmetic. They get to know the customs and procedures of their school, town and country. They acquire a position in groups and clubs.

In their high-school days children get to know their own needs and skills. They learn what they can do well, where their affinities lie. Their education gains a direction, through their own electives, with which they can later go out into the world.

3. A much smaller-scale example: toddlers learn to eat and drink, then they learn to eat what they are given, and only then come individual preferences.

For children's physical, psychological and spiritual health, it's necessary that these phases are gone through well and in the right sequence. We can observe this through the metaphor of a building: the foundation is the rock-solid certainty that we are members of a group of beings on earth who call themselves and each other 'human beings'. All members of this group call themselves 'I'. Being an 'I', a self, is what makes us human beings. If this identification with being human has been achieved well, it's easier to experience and treat our fellow people as human beings later in life – and not, for example, as a type or subspecies (man, woman, Christian, Jew, Muslim). The best protection against group discrimination does not lie in national campaigns but in quietly learning the needs and skills of being human.

On the first storey of our building the space already gets smaller. There is the certain, though still unconscious, awareness that we are part of a family, a neighbourhood. The people with whom we belong live on this first storey. The question of whether we are happy in this environment is not yet asked; it's simply given that we as children speak the language, or perhaps languages, of our fellow humans. We adopt the customs of this group as a matter of course, and in this phase they fit us like a glove. This connection with our family, with our compatriots, is for many people the most important reason to keep going when faced with the trials of life. As human beings we are fellow human beings, and language makes this possible. But being a fellow human being can be very difficult; when one group feels superior to the other, conflict is born. This is why quarrelling in childhood is so important: it teaches children how to resolve disputes.

All human beings who become themselves also get to know loneliness, which strikes the moment children realise their uniqueness. A ten-year-old may worry: 'Maybe nobody thinks like I do, maybe I'm the only one seeing this.' Young people don't lose this feeling of being unique and lonely in adolescence. On the second storey human beings are with themselves, which is not without risk. On this storey it's all about me and not about others. From this position children can say to their parents and to the world, 'I am my own boss.' To which we may think, 'If only that were true...' (Better to hang on to this thought than say it out loud!)

When are we safe on the storey of the self? This question can be answered using insights into the development of attachment. Two themes are very important here: attachment and trust. By *attachment* I mean that the first two phases have been experienced well. By *trust* I mean the certainty that we have a place in the broader context of life, that we matter.

Being ourselves

In order to effectively be ourselves, we need to develop human solidarity, which I will break down into three themes that, not coincidentally, relate to the previous section.

- ♠ Duty and the struggle to become free of its grasp
- ♠ Connectedness and its cultivation
- ♠ Freedom and learning how to handle it

Duty

A duty is involuntary. Eating is a duty: if we don't eat, we'll die. The same goes for sleeping and drinking. Duty is about staying alive, taking care of our basic physical obligations. Parenting is full of duties: as a parent we are obligated to… Life is full of duties: if we work here, we are obligated to… If we do not respond before the first of the month, we are obligated to… Duty is coercion and we want to struggle out of its grasp. Duty stands in the way of connectedness and freedom. So if we get rid of duties are we free? It's not quite that simple, because there are sanctions on failure to comply with duties. Besides which, if people don't comply with their duties, their life becomes a mess. Duties give rights: 'If you do what I obligate you to do, you will get a reward.' Stated in this way, this seems a strange point of departure in parenting, but this is often what parenting amounts to.

So, which duties do we comply with and which do we try to wriggle out of? The things we encounter as duties in life call on us to make choices. Either we say yes to the duty and we do it joyfully, in which case it is no longer a duty; or we submit to the duty and reap the reward; or we decide the duty does not apply to us and we go our own way.

Connectedness

Connectedness is quite different. It involves feeling so closely related to other people that we can feel and act on their behalf. The word 'love' would fit here as well. Love is something that increases when we share it; in the realm of love we become richer when we give. There are a couple of obvious areas where we can practise connectedness. The bond most parents experience with their children is based on connectedness (or love). This is quite different from 'liking' or feeling 'sympathy'. Love is the reason most parents of unsettled babies who never get to sleep through the night don't throw their children out! Children are also connected with their parents in this unconditional manner, and in a sense also with their brothers and sisters. With them we learn that we are unconditionally connected to human beings who we can also find immensely annoying!

Another situation in which we develop connectedness is, of course, being in love. Being in love may make us blind, but it also makes us clairvoyant. Love makes it possible to look through the outside and see the hidden inside: we want to merge with each other, be absorbed by each other, and are willing to do anything to be with each other. That is the power of being in love, and that's why some people get addicted to it. For many people the feeling of being in love ebbs away and is replaced by faithfulness. Faithfulness is also a form of more or less unconditional connectedness.

We can measure the stature of people's humanity by the extent of their circle of connectedness. People with a large circle of connectedness are peacemakers. Why is it so difficult to expand our circle in this way? Why don't we all have a large circle? It could after all be a way to peace. I think the most important reason is that we assume responsibility for people we take into our circle of connectedness. For example, a girl might stick up for her little brother in the playground, whereas at home he's a brat and she won't go near him. In the same way we feel responsible – no, we are responsible – for the people in our circle. Parents acquire this responsibility, which rests on trust, through the birth of their child. A similar trust is necessary for real connectedness.

Freedom

When children have wrested themselves free from duty, when they have found a circle of friends with whom they are unconditionally connected, it's time to taste freedom. Only then.

Exercising freedom is a new area. It doesn't fit in the area of duty, nor in the area of love. Freedom is the crown on the project of becoming yourself as a human being. Freedom has no place in the realm of rights and duties, even though we use the word freedom in that context, e.g., a nation that frees itself from the yoke of an authoritarian regime.

Freedom plays a subordinate role in the realm of connectedness. We can only take someone into our circle in freedom, which does not come automatically. It must be won by grasping it from limiting threats, such as the galling bonds of the environment in which we grew up, the limitations imposed by an illness, or the terror of psychosis in our soul. By conquering such resistance we do not become free but strong, just as immunity increases by conquering an illness. Strength is an acquisition of the body (immunity) or the soul (being able to get through difficult times). Freedom is an acquisition of the spirit.

Are there areas in which we can practise freedom, as there are for connectednesss – in which our children can exercise their freedom safely?

I see three:

🏠 Original thinking

- 🏠 Inspiration in the emotional realm
- 🏠 Selflessness in actions

These are big words, but children practise them on a small scale.

ORIGINALITY

When children aged ten realise, 'No one else thinks like I do,' they may be looking at their own thinking from the outside, as it were, for the first time. Every able human being can do this. I am free to investigate and organise my thoughts – to decide which are useful, which I've borrowed from others, which are imitative and which are original. Children learn this in school, certainly in adolescence: the fun of thinking, of examining one's own thoughts.

INSPIRATION

There is no art without inspiration. Artistic design begins with learning technical skills, but soon it also has to involve inspiration. Children learn to ask the questions: With what or whom am I so connected that I feel inspired?

SELFLESSNESS

The most difficult of the three is appropriating freedom in the realm of daily life. The most important question here can be: what does the situation ask of me? The answer to this question encompasses both external and internal factors. External: what is the situation, what's going on, what actions would help to move it a step forward? Internal: what are my capacities, what is the best I can offer? I briefly touched on this area when speaking of transforming duty into intention. We are most free when realising freedom through our actions: acting purely for the good of the situation. For many people this is not a daily experience, but I think many people are capable of doing it. For example, in raising children, there are moments when we may think: 'I know what I'm doing, I'm doing it for love – that's what's driving me forward.'

Chapter 5.
Images

When I look in the mirror, I don't doubt for a moment that the person looking back really exists. When that person smiles I don't think, 'It's only a mirror, is he really smiling?' Nor do I when that person looks sleepy and tired. The image in the mirror is nevertheless a virtual image. That virtual image stands just as far behind the mirror as I stand in front of it. When I walk backwards, my mirror image does the same. It is never the other way around. We are firmly linked to one another. The initiative lies in the real world, the virtual image follows.

It's interesting that the term 'virtual' has been chosen for the images on TV and computer screens: real, yet not real. Where does the initiative lie? Let's first take an intermediate step to another image: the photo.

Photographs

If I position the camera just right, I can take a photo of myself and also of my mirror image. If I've positioned the mirror correctly and the photo comes out well, I can no longer see which image is me and which is the mirror image: the difference between original and virtual falls away. Then I look at one of the photos. What am I looking at? It's clear that I'm looking at an image. The reality of the photo as such is paper, pigments, chemicals. Yet it speaks to me because it's a picture of reality. But I can only experience this if I recreate the image within myself. With the photo as a starting point I create within myself a reality that I can observe and experience. On the basis of a photo I remember how it was back then. I feel the sun on my skin and the wind in my ears. Should we also call that representation a virtual image? Is the photo actually 'behind the mirror'? We are not used to calling photos virtual images, but there is something to be said for it. It is indeed comparable to the extent that the photo corresponds one-to-one to the original like the mirror image corresponds with the person in front of the mirror. But there is also a significant difference. I do not need to use my imagination to look into a real mirror: the image is obtrusively true. Looking at a photo requires imagination, otherwise we see nothing.

Images from nature

There are therefore various kinds of images: mirror images, virtual images, photographs. Their similarity is that they point to an original. The difference lies in the creative imagination that is or is not needed to recognise that the image is an image. The phenomenon that something can be an image of something else is quite commonplace. Nature is full of it.

The arrival of buds in spring is an image of new life. It *is* new life, but it's also an image or representation of it. The falling of leaves in autumn is an image of withdrawing life. It both *is* that and an image or representation of it. Shadows lengthening in the evening is an image of internalisation, of withdrawing inward. Lighting a fire is an image of being warmed – that is what it means for the person in front of the fire, but for the fire it may mean something quite different: the reality is that wood is burning.

When we observe in amazement how an oak tree thrusts its branches into space, we see power! How different from a birch or other trees. We may be certain that with every phenomenon we observe in the natural world we have not only a sensory observation (colour, form, smell), it also tells us something about its characteristics, if we are interested. It presents an image of something that lies within it. If we go through nature observing it in this way it becomes, as it were, transparent. Nature can, as Goethe describes it, unveil its public secret to us.[26]

I have used nature as an example because everyone has experience of it. Everyone who has been in the woods or on the beach, has cycled against the wind or has sat next to a waterfall, knows the eloquence and depth encompassed within natural objects – hence the expression, 'Say it with flowers.' When we give someone a bouquet of flowers, we think about the message we want the bouquet to convey. If we're hoping to make amends for something, we may buy red tulips, but red roses would be a bit over the top.

Screen images

To what extent are screen images really images in the true sense of the word, as described above? Are they virtual images from 'behind the mirror'? It depends somewhat on whether the image being represented really existed at some point or whether imaginary beings have been constructed.

Back when a movie still consisted of an enormous number of photos, we were dealing with the principle of photography and the illusion of movement. Photography originated from a reality that existed or had been constructed in the studio. The slowness of the eye caused us to 'observe' movement. We did in fact add the movement in our imagination and then observe it. When sound could be played alongside the film it became even easier to follow the story. This meant that we first constructed the story in our imagination and then were touched by it.

Now that films are recorded and played digitally, we have taken a step towards alienation. The relationship between the digital image (created in binary: zeros and ones) and the original reality has been bypassed. Only when the zeros and ones are turned into coloured pixels, which in turn are combined into moving shapes, do we recognise (assuming the decoding has gone well) the images of the situation that was once filmed. What is remarkable about this technical tour de force is that it seems more real than old-fashioned films, whereas in reality the deconstruction of the original image goes much further than with celluloid film. In old-fashioned photos and films images came about through silver nitrate or another light-sensitive substances; in digital media substance barely plays a role.

The detachment of screen images from reality is taken a step further when moving images are construed of things (nature, people, animals and beings) that don't really exist. The creative imagination of the maker designs a reality. That reality doesn't remain in the personal inner world of the maker, as is the case when people dream or watch a film. The maker's imagined reality is projected outward, so that images of nature, people, animals and beings become visible on the screen. Who could have surmised a hundred years ago that people would be able to actualise their dreams?

What kinds of images are they, from what do they derive their 'reality'? Because they are real in a certain way. So real that they drag thousands of young gamers into realms that were hitherto unknown, realms in which the gamers live, act and have emotions. But in the sensory world, the world most people call the 'real world', no corresponding image can be found. This type of virtual on-screen image has no corresponding reality this side of the mirror. In my opinion there can be no other conclusion than that the reality comes into being in the consciousness of the viewer. The on-screen medium creates a new reality and the stage for this reality is the consciousness of the spectator. Perhaps we shouldn't use the term 'virtual image' then: the word 'virtual' at least suggests a mirrored reality. 'Illusory images' seems more fitting.

'So what?' you may ask. Is that new, or exceptional, or even bad? It is certainly a novelty that new realities are produced in people on this scale and so intrusively. It is not daydreaming, in which people fill their own inner world with their own new images. It is bad to the extent that it is virtually impossible to avoid these new realities. Zeros and ones use my imagination, my expressive capacity to let images emerge in my inner world. Children certainly cannot escape from this coercive effect. It is an imagination that's forced upon them. Just as calculators do not help children learn to do mental arithmetic, so virtual images do not help them to develop an imagination. And that is bad. For without imagination a person cannot think and remember.

Chapter 6.
Art

What is art?

You have probably stood in front of a work of art, particularly modern art, and asked yourself, 'How is this art?' What distinguishes one artefact from another? What makes something art?

Most people agree that Picasso was an artist. Does that mean everything Picasso made was art? Or to bring the question closer to home: when are we ourselves artists? When we find the perfect vase for the flowers we picked and set them in the ideal spot to catch the light and really enhance the room – are we artists? Can we awaken the artist within when we have a conversation with our partner, our child, our friend? Can conversation be art?

Since this book is about parenting, let's ask the question differently. At what age can children enjoy art? What level of maturity must we achieve to recognise a work of art as art? Imagine the scene: a group of children in a museum with a teacher who's explaining the work of art they're looking at, or at least sitting in front of – well-intentioned but pointless. We can see at a single glance that the children are not seeing a work of art. Unless… The children can be interested in the technique, the use of colour, the perspective, the motifs and possibly in the meaning of the painting, for example, an allegory of vanity. One or two children may recognise the emotion that's represented. But do they understand it as a work of art? Unless one of the group is touched by something: 'Miss, I wonder what that man's thinking. Maybe he's sad because he's lost something.' When this kind of question arises, the teacher can join in and a dialogue can develop: 'He's just resting.' 'You can see he's rich.' 'Maybe he's lonely?'

These kinds of questions enliven the situation, setting in motion a process in which the colours and forms become, as it were, transparent. From behind the canvas come questions and answers, meanings that dissolve again. A work of art never has only one single level of interpretation. In the process of searching we can peel off the layers and come to the core. Or perhaps it's not the core but the art's magnificence that constitutes its actual meaning?

We look and ask, we listen, taste and feel. When contemplating art, we do not use our senses in the usual manner: we bring our senses to life by letting them collaborate and ask questions.[27]

Must a work of art be contemplated to be art? A stage play without an audience, an exhibition without visitors, a statue that has been lost at sea – are they art? Or conversely: can we make things into art if we look at them with artistic vision? Even something common like a fork, or something ugly like kitsch? How can we stop ourselves from being distracted by the common or ugly, so we can see beauty underneath? Or perhaps 'beauty' is not the right concept? Perhaps what matters is that the item touches us, that we are touched by the truth of it? Are we touched by the inspiration that caused the artist to create the work of art?

Children's art

All children draw, paint and model with clay whenever they have a chance. Often they are peacock-proud of their creations: 'For you, Mum' and Mum wonders if she can find it beautiful and exclaims something like, 'Thank you, you have made this wonderfully'. What do we do with it? Do we put it away in a cupboard, let it lie about, pin it on the fridge, frame it? Do we treat it like a gift or a work of art? Is it a work of art?

In a sense it is. When young children draw or paint they are at one with their work, which is nothing out of the ordinary, of course. Under normal conditions, children are always at one with their work. Tying shoelaces, eating an apple and drawing are activities children not only *do*; children *are* what they are doing in that moment. Their entire being is involved in that action; they are inspired. This is why things children make sometimes have such an elemental expressiveness: they are expressions of their mode of being at that moment.[28] In that sense they

85

are art: children's art. Viewed in this way the process of growing up is art in itself, because children gradually become visible, they become manifest, they unfold, they unwrap. Their creations on paper and from other materials are part of this. Put abstractly: something from the invisible spiritual world becomes manifest in the visible world. And with this we are very close to a description of art.

Children's art has no eternal value; it is an expression of a particular moment in the story of the development of a particular child. Therefore, hang it up and replace it after a few days. Put it on the windowsill, then in the cupboard after a week, and let it quietly disappear after a month.

Why is art so important in life?

Being artistically and creatively active, and observing artistically, are activities that raise people above everyday existence and thereby make us more human. Through art people gain access to a world that wants to become visible, a world behind the canvas, behind the clay and the colour. It is hugely beneficial for children to learn to express themselves creatively and to observe artistically. By seeing behind the canvas they can learn a lot about the world, about things other than the merely practical. While children must learn practical skills to cope in everyday life, children who have also learned to investigate context, motivation and inspiration can orient themselves more easily in this confusing world.

What is there to be seen 'behind' LCD screens? What lies behind the images on TV and computers? Can we also gain access to those images in an artistic way? This is not an easy question, but as far as I'm concerned it's the central question of this book, which I will investigate more closely in Chapter 8.

Chapter 7.
Play

When Goethe said, 'More precious than gold is the light and more invigorating than the light is conversation,'[29] I think he overlooked children's play, or he saw it as a form of conversation. What on earth is more beautiful than a child undisturbed at play? As if from nothing children develop a stream of images, ideas, decisions, and twists and turns. The flowering season of the imagination, of fantasy games, lies roughly between the ages of two-and-a-half and five. Some children use materials for their play, whatever is at hand. A block that first was a boat is moments later a drowning victim to be rescued. A pinecone is quite as easily a tree in a field as a cow in a pasture. Children change substances effortlessly. They bend reality to their will and create new worlds. But their fantasy land is anything but arbitrary: everything happens according to a plan that didn't exist before but manifests itself in the course of playing. Elements of daily life intertwine with fairy-tale and dream worlds. These self-created realities hold as much joy as children have within them and as much fear as they can bear. Through play children bolster their health, they digest indigestible impressions, and practise steadfastness and persistence. In their play world children are wonderfully cared for and they bring about happy endings.

When we watch children undisturbed at play, we can observe an artistic process of creating balance and healing. Children bear whole-making powers within themselves; they experience them in their expressive imagination and make them come true in play, which they express through images. In this process they can explore and deal with issues – intervene and direct. Play images are like children's drawings: images of a reality, but fuller, more dynamic, more transitory.

Children's play is not stage play, not make-believe. Only much later, somewhere in adolescence, can young people really play-act. Although in Steiner-Waldorf schools every Class 6 ends the year with a play in which the children perform and play a role. But that's not what I mean by play-acting, in which children must identify with another character. That can only happen when we have become our own self to some degree (see pp.67–76). Then performing on stage helps us find our own self in contrast to the character we are playing. Children's play is no stage play, it is reality. It is life itself, a serious exercise of life and death, joy and sadness. Through play children activate their own imagination and their health-giving, restorative powers.

What is play?

You may wonder whether this panegyric to play applies to all children's play or perhaps even to everything children undertake spontaneously. I don't think that's the case; there are gradations. Ludo and Stratego are games in which imagination plays a lesser role. Games such as tag, hide-and-seek and pétanque come closer, in which aspects of life such as being cunning, grasping the overall picture, looking ahead and winning and losing can be practised without a feeling of being threatened by the results. But the most significant form of play is truly free play: a child alone or with one, two or three others, where imagination takes the lead role, rules emerge and fade away again on the spot; play in which adults have no say.

From about age ten children forget how to play like this, to their great sorrow as they grow older; prepubescent children often experience nostalgia for play. But they can no longer do it: the sun of the creative imagination sets, the light of the so-called real world is turned on. Twelve-year-olds can for a time still play with their little brothers or sisters, but they know: I am playing at playing.

You may wonder whether videogames and electronic toys fall under the topic of play. This is, after all, a book about screen time and parenting. I don't think they do – to the contrary – which is the topic of the next two chapters.

Chapter 8.
Genuine vs. Virtual

One important task of parenting is to teach children to distinguish between genuine and simulated. Genuine silk is very different from artificial silk or rayon. This may sound like a matter of course, but think, for example, of a masterpiece by a famous painter that at some point is unmasked as a forgery. Thousands of people have enjoyed it in ignorance, nevertheless we believe the difference between the genuine masterpiece and the forgery is important.

Or conversely, when we go to see an illusionist perform, we know beforehand that we're being skilfully hoodwinked. We choose the illusion and pay for it.

Although it may seem obvious that we uphold a strict separation between make-believe and real, in the digital era the two intermingle and sometimes change places. We could claim that this lack of clarity creates a central problem when raising children. Let me give four examples:

- ♠ virtual sound
- ♠ virtual encounters
- ♠ virtual images
- ♠ virtual play

Virtual sound

In his 1964 mini masterpiece on the influence of radio and television on toddlers and young children, Fritz Wilmar claimed that mechanically produced sound is 'pseudo sound'.[30] He explained that when sound is reduced to electromagnetic vibrations by recording equipment its essence is lost and is not reborn when replayed through amplifiers and speakers. What Wilmar explained for his day, of course, applies even more strongly to the reduction of sound to zeros and ones (binary code) in digital recording and reproduction. Sound is maximally estranged from its essence, while modern technology suggests the opposite: perfect illusion, glamorous ersatz. In the early twentieth century the notion gained ground that sound is a purely physical phenomenon, merely vibrations. This is a perfect example of what in the development of science is called 'nothing butterism' – reducing a phenomenon to its physical characteristics.[31]

No one will deny that for sound to occur there must be vibrations in the air, but our daily experience contradicts the claim that vibrations are the only factor involved in sound production and that they constitute its essence. When a song sticks in my head, or when I relive a concert or make a song up myself, it happens without sound vibrations. Sound waves are the carrier of the 'message' the tones convey, not the essence. When music expresses sorrow or cheerfulness, the sorrow or cheerfulness cause the sounds, not the reverse.

Children discover that sounds are hidden within matter in a very simple way. They hit the table with a spoon or the bars of the playpen with a block, or they splash bath water with their hand. Promptly a miracle appears: sound is liberated from substance. It's an elementary experience for every hearing child: sound is hidden in substance and we must do something to conjure it out.

It's not difficult to put together an orchestra at home with homemade instruments, and children can learn important lessons in this way. To name a few: that something essential is hidden in objects; that we must become active to find this out; that sounds have an effect; that sounds can harmonise; that we must wait our turn; that the whole is more than the sum of the parts; that something essential happens in silence. Instruments can be refined so that the specific properties of wood, silver and copper are made to sound.

Looked at, or rather listened to, in this way, sound emitted by a speaker is always an illusion, a simulated sound. It does not let the inner quality of the material of the speaker or the headphone sound. It has been referred to as 'canned' or 'tinned' sound, which actually gives it more due than it deserves. Beans in a tin still have a great deal to do with the original beans from nature; sound in a tin no longer has anything to do with the original sounds: it is merely imitation, perfect falsification.

It may be interesting to think about how many real tones and how much imitation sound surround our children each day. Is it bad to be surrounded by imitation sound? Yes, it's bad, especially in the case of sound, because sound is made to reveal something inward, something essential. Imitation sounds take this experience away from children. Can we do something to combat this? Yes, of course: we can counterbalance virtual sound with plenty of opportunities to experience real sound (see Chapter 11, p.120).

Virtual encounters

Children become themselves through their encounters with other people (see pp.67–76). Children need their parents, brothers and sisters, grandparents, classmates and so on. It's not only encounters with people that are important; children experience all kinds of encounters, and the more real they are, the more children benefit from them. By colliding with a solid object, for example, children learn that they're not as solid! They get up and become more skilful in finding their way. From encounters with nature, for example by experiencing the seasons in a park, children learn that they are related to nature: they too go through a process and that requires time.

Through encounters with animals, for example a pet or earthworms in the garden, children learn tenderness, care, wonder, fear and other emotions. They learn that there's a world around them populated by all kinds of beings going about their own business.

From encounters with people children learn to know themselves. They learn that other people call themselves 'I' and that they can do the same. They learn that they are the centre of their own universe and that they can share that universe with other people.

Becoming themselves is ultimately the greatest achievement parents can hope their children will fulfil; becoming themselves in a world that supports them, to which they feel connected and in which they share responsibility.

Real encounters are irreplaceable: really falling and bumping, really getting wet in the rain, really being surprised by a butterfly, really looking someone in the eye. Virtual encounters lead nowhere. The physical confrontation with a screen, experiencing nature by watching a film, encountering animals through *Bambi*, chatting to a friend through messaging: all this leads nowhere. I hear the objections: these things are instructive, entertaining, convenient and easy. Of course they are, but compared to an encounter they are a waste of time. Do digital media provide any valuable function? They certainly do: they can be instructive, entertaining, convenient and easy, but they do not lead to an encounter.

This is the moment to say something about the sense

of self.[32] Understanding the sense of self makes it clear why there can be no true encounter other than finding ourselves with another person in the same physical space. Like the sense of touch, the sense of self allows us to observe that there's a reality that belongs to me as well as a reality that doesn't belong to me, which is not 'I'. The sense of touch is inborn. All healthy children learn through the sense of touch that they have a physical body with which to distinguish themselves from the outside world.

The sense of self is not inborn. Originally babies and young children are at one with their environment, with the familiar people in their environment to be exact. Gradually children begin to distinguish themselves from the people close to them. Being naughty helps tremendously in this process. Calling themself 'I' is a milestone on children's path towards becoming their self. Children only truly realise at about age nine that they are really different from all other people. Before this they will have known for a long time that other people behave differently, but only now do they realise that other people are indeed 'others', and they learn this through their sense of self. Children use their sense of self to distinguish between Dad's bad mood and Dad himself. They know in a flash whether Mum says something out of habit or really means it. The difference is: in the latter case Mum is really present in her self. This is an observation, not reasoning or a conclusion. The sense of self must be trained or it will not function. Without real encounters of the self, the capacity languishes. A well-trained sense of self is necessary to distinguish real from fake. Are you really this person? Are you real? These are questions the sense of self can answer. How should we encourage our children to develop their sense of self? Quite simply by ensuring *our* self is really present in our interactions, as training material for our child's sense of self. Facebook, Skype and Instagram serve other purposes, but they are not training grounds for the sense of self.

Virtual images

In Chapter 5 we looked at different kinds of pictures, moving and non-moving, which we call images. The reality content of these images varies greatly.

Here I want to say something about visual and auditory perceptions, which differ fundamentally from one another. The difference is significant in terms of the effect of these means of perception on growing children. Stated succinctly, we can formulate the difference as follows: in auditory perceptions the content is included; in visual perceptions the content remains hidden. This statement requires clarification.[33]

Sound externalises something that was first inwardly hidden. The sound is both the content of sensory perception as well as the meaning. It's quite different with perception via the eye. We look by definition at the outside of things, their appearance. Objects show themselves in their colour and form, but we don't learn anything about their inner being. When we look at a flowering plant, a dandelion or a poppy or a cornflower, for example, we can ask: What kind of thing are you? What are you like inside – your vitality, your taste, your healing power? To find answers to these questions we must do something: study the plant, perhaps taste it, smell it, read about it. Gradually the plant becomes familiar to us and exposes its inner being. Then we discover, for example, that it's not coincidental that dandelions are yellow, poppies red and cornflowers blue. The colours speak a language – and words are derived from the auditory world. When we find out about something's content, it begins to sound – there is speech.

The appearance of natural objects is not accidental, but we have to take another action in order to hear them speak. This is true of nature, but not necessarily of manmade objects. Almost anything can be imitated with synthetic materials such as plastic, but the outward appearance is by no means an image of the 'inside' content. Take artificial flowers, for example. The development of synthetic materials has a great many consequences, an important one being that the visual information surrounding children accustoms them to counterfeits in the visible world.

The move towards virtual images, as mentioned in Chapter 5 – the simulated images of the flat screen – is a huge step both quantitatively and qualitatively. Any relationship between the visual image and the reality behind it has been eliminated. The reality is a screen with light-emitting elements that can be switched on and off. The content is formed in the consciousness of the person watching the screen. Understood in this sense, screen images are not merely simulated images, but anti-images, which we will discuss further in Chapter 9.

Why are virtual images so bad for children? For the following reason: in order for children to develop fully, so they can grow up to help the world progress healthily, they must be able to see beneath the surface of phenomena. We must encourage them to develop an open ear for what has not yet been spoken, and an open eye for what can be seen behind the facts. Many modern children are born with an aptitude for this. They are in some way clairvoyant or clairaudient: they hear what we actually mean through what we say. This can go so far that they see the hidden creative and therapeutic forces in nature. We can either extinguish or develop this aptitude through our parenting. Children must, of course, live in the modern world, which means using digital media, but we should also be aware, as parents, that too much screen time can extinguish their aptitude for 'seeing beyond', and this must not happen.

Virtual play

In an article dealing with the question of privacy a Dutch daily newspaper recently wrote: 'Google and Facebook pounce on children.'[34] The internet appears to be one great play paradise, offering information and entertainment and various things in-between (sometimes called edutainment), all for free. In the meantime children's play behaviour is being monitored, and in no time at all Google know more about how our children learn than we do as parents.

'Mum, may I go on the computer?' usually means: may I play a video game? They may also have unlimited access to games on their own tablet or smartphone. From about twelve years old, it's highly likely that children, especially boys, will get to know the world of gaming. With their friends, or with virtual friends, they deploy their astuteness and intelligence in defeating monsters, eliminating opponents and unlocking secret rooms. According to Clive Thompson, this is making our children ever smarter.[35] He explains that in the process of playing video games, they learn to solve problems intuitively, and when playing with friends, they learn that we can find a solution more quickly through collaboration. He believes that the sooner children become acquainted with this way of problem solving, the better, as it equips them for a place in the modern digital multimedia world.

I'm afraid Clive Thompson is right. By doing sums we get better at maths, by gaming we become better gamers. The question is whether that's the future we have in mind for our children; whether that will enable them to leave the world a better place than they found it.

In this context let's ask whether video games bring the same results as playing off screen. The answer is, of course, no. Real play is guided by children's imaginations; virtual games are guided by their designer's imagination. Real play has a future, virtual play only a past. In the real world cheating is a real possibility; in the virtual world cheating is only possible when that possibility has been built in. Otherwise it's a design error, a fault that must be rectified as soon as possible.

Manfred Spitzer has provided support for the thesis that virtual games do not make children more, but rather less, intelligent.[36] It depends, of course, on how we define intelligence. If we consider 'intelligence' to mean the ability to rapidly collect facts and remember them for a short period of time, he is wrong. But if we consider it to mean using our experience and knowledge to face problems and to arrive at creative solutions, his claim is right.

Play helps children to order their world and to make it understandable; real play, that is. Making music also helps a great deal, and sleeping. When children get too little sleep they become cranky, they can no longer play or learn well. What should we do to encourage our children to play? The answer is simple: don't entertain them; allow boredom to strike. Healthy children won't stand that for long; they will go and play.

Chapter 9.
Anti-parenting

Just as there are virtual variants of certain phenomena, so there are anti-variants, which we'll discuss in this chapter. It's important to be aware of these when raising children because they are factors that completely contradict our parenting intentions. If we recognise them we can do something about them, but if we don't we're defenceless. The three anti-variants I'm referring to are:

- 🏠 anti-time
- 🏠 anti-encounter
- 🏠 anti-freedom

Anti-time

In his fantasy novel *Momo*, Michael Ende described what happens when time is stolen[37]. Anyone who regularly uses the internet will know this from personal experience: we suddenly realise we've spent two hours online without achieving what we intended to do, and we feel quite ashamed for wasting that time. Yes, it's possible to lose time, and Michael Ende described it well. When we sleep we also lose time, or when we're daydreaming or lost in a book.

To understand how this can happen let's consider the phenomenon of time further. The concept of 'stealing time' becomes self-evident when we realise that time is not something abstract but rather something extremely concrete. The primal phenomenon of our sense of time is the experience of day and night. We develop not only because of our daytime experiences, but also because we process those experiences when we're sleeping at night.

During the day, when we're fully conscious, time passes according to the logic of the clock: it's either morning, afternoon or evening. By the end of the day, we're one day older than we were at the same time yesterday.

At night it's quite different. If we experience time in our dreams, it's simultaneous: we can look around in time-space. It's not timelessness, as we often find ourselves somewhere in time. But time is wherever our attention is. Sometimes the direction of time seems to be reversed. The sound that wakes us up can feature at the end of our dream narrative; the conclusion of the story already existed in the physical world before the dream began.

The alternation of day and night keeps us healthy and allows us to develop. After one bad night's sleep our alertness, reaction speed, creativity and learning ability are significantly undermined. After a few bad nights' sleep we become zombies. Structured time therefore doesn't play a passive role: it's an active force; time does something to us. It forms the basis of our consciousness and memory. Without structured time there would be no development.

All processes take place within time. Let's consider this in relation to plants. During the day they photosynthesise; at night they grow in darkness. We can assess what influences time (length of the day, temperature and season) has on the formation of plants, on their development, flowering, fructification and the formation of seeds.

Time processes are life processes. The sun is 'time giver' and the giver of all life. There's a reason why the day-night rhythm forms the basis of life on earth. If we want to stay healthy, a rhythmic life is necessary, and Father Time is the guarding, sustaining, protective force that enables rhythm.

And now back to *Momo*, in which Michael Ende showed that time is endangered. Not clock time, but the sustaining time that makes life possible. Father Time apparently has an opponent – anti-time – which has been at work when we feel as if we've wasted time: we've lost a little bit of our self and inhibited our development.

In her *Harry Potter* books, J.K. Rowling based her 'Dementors' on a similar phenomenon. She imagined what effect these memory eaters could have on a modern child like Harry Potter, sucking the life from him and causing a paralysing, overwhelming fear. But more ordinary, less magically endowed children like our own are also sensitive to anti-time. Anti-time is not the exclusive province of digital media, of course, but dealing with digital media has made anti-time a worldwide reality that we experience daily.

Anti-encounter

In Chapter 8 we considered how encounters provide essential opportunities for becoming human (see p.94). Children become themselves through their encounters with other people. These encounters don't necessarily have to be pleasant or even positive; self-awareness is gained through observing the unfamiliar and non-related. Children need to experience resistance in encounters in order to learn how to defend their boundaries. Relatedness does not automatically mean sympathy, nor the reverse. When considering human solidarity, we ask the question: Which people belong to my circle (whether I consider them sympathetic or not)?

We can ask the question: Do I have the right to exclude people from my circle? Are there people on this earth whom I reject on principle, whom I do not wish to encounter? In the stories presented daily in newspapers, on radio and TV, it appears that many people have answered this question with: 'Yes, there are people I reject on principle, which gives me the right to despise, humiliate and kill them.' There can, of course, be decisive reasons to disdain people and to wage war, for example, based on a sense of justice: someone attacks our territory. But on another level – the level of becoming our self as a human being – such aggression offers no contribution. To the contrary, it has the opposite (anti) effect.

You may be wondering how this relates to the theme of this book. Children see a considerable amount of violence in the scenes they watch on screen. In detective programmes, they regularly witness murders, which become a fact of life. In children's cartoons, characters are literally beaten to a pulp, only to spring back to life in the next scene. The goal of many children's video games is to get rid of as many opponents as possible – often aliens, who apparently don't matter. Sometimes figures are depicted very realistically, and they're very realistically blown to pieces.

We could ask: What's wrong with suspense and excitement? Didn't most men play soldiers when they were young? Through these multimedia experiences children are being taught contempt for the existence of others, which is bad. They also become either fascinated by or afraid of violence: it works both ways. The mix of fear and violence is exceptionally explosive, as everyone knows.

We could say: 'They know quite well that it's just a game. Playing violent games allows them to get rid of their aggression in a harmless way.' When they buy aggressive games for their children or allow them to play them online, parents fall back on this kind of argument, based on homespun psychology. If only it were true. Hate and aggression grow when we practise them, whether offline or online – incidentally, just like love.

'Anti-encounter' is daily fare for millions of children, young people and adults all over the world. It breeds contempt for people and leads to war. It takes, on average, ten years after the introduction of TV and films into a society for the number of violent crimes to double.[38] But digital media are a fact of our society so we will have to learn to live with their side effects and turn them to the good.

Anti-freedom

When people are asked what they most value in life, they tend to say health and freedom. Almost no one says responsibility, even though it's the twin brother of freedom. Personal freedom is a relatively recent concept. In the era of the Enlightenment in eighteenth-century Europe, the influence of the church and state on our private lives was reduced to what we consider more reasonable proportions. In many parts of the world, personal freedom and autonomy are not a matter of course – the family, the community or the police are in charge, even behind closed doors. Why do we consider personal freedom to be so important? Why do we respect the 'Keep Out' sign our ten year old puts on the door of his room? Why are we so proud when our teenage daughter comes up with her own ideas? Why do we rebel when anyone, no matter whom, tells us what to think or do?

Because we live in a society in which conforming to a group is no longer as important as it used to be. Along the path to maturity we discover independently whether we believe in a God, in human kindness, whether we're vegetarian, whether we choose to buy Fair Trade goods or travel by plane, and so on. We feel responsible for making these kinds of moral decisions ourselves, so we need the freedom to choose which are good and which are bad. We feel justified in making these kinds of decisions, but we can only do so when we have developed sufficient confidence to make good decisions and are able to bear the consequences of making bad decisions.

We can't make all our decisions in isolation. An enormous counselling culture has sprung up, where people with relevant qualifications, or people who believe they've been inspired by higher powers, offer advice to others. People are searching for verification of their moral choices… but against what standard?

When we enter the realm of freedom it becomes necessary to consider good and evil, which leads us to the spiritual dimension. To experience personal freedom we have to be able to open our hearts to sources from the spiritual world. In saying this, I don't mean we need to be religious or holy. Dedicated materialists can pursue freedom by opening their hearts to materialism as a worldview – a spiritual movement (see p.23).

You may ask whether we should aspire to such a freedom. The answer is yes, for two reasons: the first is that our times call for individuals to grow towards freedom. This is simply how it is. The second, more important reason is that people can only make choices from a position of freedom, from which they are able to identify evil, find their own position and turn it to the good. Freedom is not without obligations; only free individuals can dedicate themselves to the improvement of the world.

Have we strayed a little too far here? After all, we're supposed to be discussing 'anti-freedom' in the context of raising kids in the digital world. Actually we haven't strayed far at all.

Apparently one of the side effects of the one-child policy in China was parents' tendency to put their children 'safely' in front of the TV or computer indoors, instead of letting them play freely outdoors where they might have an accident. This is not a good step towards developing freedom. In Chapter 4 I mentioned a newspaper article about the freedom of movement of four generations. When he was eight Great-grandfather was allowed to go fishing 6 miles (10 km) from home, whereas at the same age his modern-day great-grandson Ed may only go 300 yards (300 m) to the end of the street. This surely limits Ed's freedom to gain valuable life experience.

Some parents seem to desire control over all aspects of their children's lives. As a reaction to this we've seen the counter-movement of 'free-range children' being established, which aims to empower children to deal with their own free space.[39] Learning to acquire freedom requires an enormous measure of trust, on the part of children as well as their parents.

Chapter 10.
Surveying the Landscape

Before we move on to the final chapter, which focuses on practical parenting advice, let's orient ourselves for a moment and, on the basis of the preceding chapters, survey the landscape of the digital age in which we're raising our children.

Virtually nowhere is out of reach of the web that invisibly spans the earth. Practically every home penetrated by our Western lifestyle has several screens. Almost all vehicles incorporate not only electricity but also electronics. More and more household appliances are equipped with programmable mini-computers and are remotely controlled. Children worldwide play with electronic toys. Thanks to digital technology, bombs can hit their target with reasonable accuracy and without too much collateral damage. We have been on the moon and are sending equipment to Mars.

Several years have passed since 1997 when Garry Kasparov, the chess grandmaster, was defeated by a computer.[40] We can ask some newly developed computers random questions on random subjects and they will answer within a few seconds. Information from all around the world lies within our reach, and an ever-increasing amount of information about our lives is made available to the world. As is true of all technological developments, the successive steps in electronic technology have been accompanied by messianic expectations: television would bring people together; computers would make life easier; the World Wide Web would bring democracy and peace; laptops would bring development to the Third World. And now it's the turn of tablets to realise promises of pleasant schools where learning is fun and students can develop their own interests.

Since the beginning of civilization humanity has developed tools. For our topic it's appropriate to consider the development of instruments, tools and machines in relation to the question: Which function of the human body do they take over or do they support? Here are a few examples, which we can supplement with our own finds:

- ♠ The wheel has by and large supplanted walking.

- ♠ Levers and pulleys have surpassed human muscle power.

- ♠ Printing has made remembering history superfluous.

- ♠ Steam engines have released forces
  that would otherwise require dozens of
  people or horses.

- ♠ Nuclear power plants and bombs have
  unleashed forces that involve the coming
  into being and the passing away of matter.

And electronics? It's fairly clear that the functioning of the nervous system has been the model for the development of electricity and electronics. The nervous system can be viewed as a system of wiring that functions according to the yes-no principle: there is either a signal or there is no signal; the nerve is at rest or it depolarises. Our entire nervous system is filled with switch centres and other mechanisms that convey stimuli.

The parallel between the nervous system and computer function is so striking that we could consider our nervous system, including our brain, to be nothing but a complex computer – a prime example of 'nothing butterism'.[31] This is entirely in keeping with the intention of one of the first computer engineers, John von Neumann, who after an intensive study of neurology resolved 'to copy a greatly simplified model of the living brain for machines that can be made by humans.'[41]

Two versions

From this point on I'm faced with a problem. I should actually be writing two versions of my recommend-ations: one for those who don't want to read about the spiritual world, and one for those who accept the existence of a spiritual world. At this point I'm unable to write one single version with which both parties can identify.

So from here on you can choose the commonly accepted version or the spiritual version. It's clear where my own choice lies: I can only consider human development in dialogue with what lies in the non-sensory world. But we must be free to make our own considerations on this point.

A commonly accepted version

After an apparently unbridled belief in the progress of computer technology, critical voices have appeared. The side effects of screen use are not negligible. Problems with concentration, sleeping, school performance and potential addiction are perhaps the most severe. It's striking that technological developments continue apace, while in the pedagogical corner, contact with nature and sufficient opportunity for off-screen play are being stressed. The theme of privacy is also being increasingly emphasised. Scientists and pedagogues are concerned about what media giants such as Google and Facebook are doing with the overwhelming mountain of data they collect about us and our children. Where is private actually still private?

Computer technology has undeniably made our lives more interesting in many respects. Modern means of information management and communications have provided us with the 'global village'.[2] But we must also take the research findings of neuroscientists seriously; they have convincingly demonstrated that unused brain functions wither and ultimately disappear. So when we outsource certain functions of our brain and memory to a machine, it has direct and ultimately irreversible consequences for our brain. Not only for our own brain and that of our children, but also for our descendants. Hereditary material that determines brain structure and function appears to change fairly rapidly. We pass on our capacities and incapacities, in part, to our children and grandchildren.[42]

An aspect of digital media that is not often discussed is the effect on the environment, specifically radiation and energy. Due to the proliferation throughout the world of transmission masts and power lines, and because we've surrounded the earth with satellites, the amount of radiation on earth has increased enormously over the past century. The impact of this is not immediately clear and cannot be measured in the short term, but theoretically it's unlikely that there has been no effect. Some scientists earnestly warn about the harmful effect of radiation on young children's brains; it could even be carcinogenic.[43]

The energy issue is topical. Due to growing economies, the demand for electricity, fuel and energy is growing explosively. Alternative sources of energy cover only a small percentage of this demand. Fossil energy sources, which are by definition finite, still provide the majority of the energy needed to power industrial and domestic technology. The production of energy from fossil fuels, as we know, has a negative impact on the environment, one effect being that the heat that's released requires cooling, which in turn requires energy and burdens the environment through warming.[44]

A spiritual version

Influences from the non-visible spiritual world have always played an important role, even when we collectively decided this was not the case. Theories that arose during the Enlightenment of the late eighteenth century revealed extraterrestrial influences, such as those of the comets, stars and the devil to be inventions of the human spirit. They also removed God, who was deemed merely an illusion, leaving only the human spirit itself to be freed of its spiritual properties, which of course then followed. In 1842 Emil Du Bois-Reymond and Ernst von Brücke[45] declared solemnly that henceforth science would only consist of phenomena that had a material explanation, accessible through experiments. From then, only a small step was required for Dick Swaab to declare that our existence is a product of our body, more precisely of our brain.[46]

I think we can conclude that we've passed through the nadir of this materialistic worldview.[47] In recent years we openly speak of mindfulness, Ayurveda, meditation and clairvoyant experiences. More and more often children and parents in the consulting room talk about their experiences in the non-sensory realm. There's a considerable volume of literature about near-death experiences that have substantially changed people's lives. And there is, of course, anthroposophy, which describes research in the spiritual world with scientific exactness. It's largely from an anthroposophical perspective that I describe the next section, which relates to the impact of digital technology on the non-visible world.

Materialism is beneficial to the extent that it has taught people to trust their own minds and observations. It is problematic to the extent that it has deprived people of a perception of their origin and destiny: the world of the spirit. Materialism is most at home in the head, the seat of consciousness, and most uncomfortable in the heart, the area of feelings. The heart's logic is that of love, like the logic of the fox in *The Little Prince*, who knew that we see most clearly when following our hearts.[48]

The processes of the 'will', which are not subject to logic and control, are entirely incomprehensible from the materialistic viewpoint. Our will is sometimes guided by something we may need in the future –

an inversion of cause and effect. Forces of the will drove the development of the tools, instruments and machines that took over from human power.

Forces of the heart have driven our restless impulse to travel, which started with the wheel and may someday end on Mars. Forces of the nervous system have been used to spread the conviction that reality is essentially material. Even from a materialistic perspective, this is not entirely correct. When we look around on earth and consider what forces are at work, we find three kinds: earthly, super-earthly and sub-earthly forces.

We are familiar with earthly forces, or we think we are: weight, density, warmth and cold, the forces of attraction and repulsion among objects and substances.

We are also familiar with super-earthly forces: the growing and flowering of plants; the influences of weather and climate.

And we are also familiar with sub-earthly forces from the underworld: electricity, magnetism, nuclear power. Sub-earthly influences have access to people and animals through our nervous systems, which function via electricity: a nerve impulse is a wave of electrical activity that passes from one end of a neuron to the other. Provided these sub-earthly influences are embedded in our whole organism, in which the heart and other organs also fulfil their roles, no difficulties should arise. As always, when this coherent balance is disturbed, when the nerves and brain take over, problems emerge.

This is precisely the situation in which we find ourselves today – due to, among other things, the development of electronic technology. There is nothing wrong with this, provided technology does not assume control. The situation is comparable to that of the sorcerer's apprentice, who has set a spell in motion then loses his grip on it, and it does its own thing. But, for us, no great sorcerer will appear and stop the process from continuing to spiral out of control: we ourselves must act. Sub-earthly forces are powerful but they have no heart – no compassion, consideration or morality with which to moderate the chain of events set in motion by the human 'sorcerer's apprentice'.

Chapter 11.
Practical Advice for Parenting in the Digital World

A commonly accepted perspective

As we have seen, digital developments have changed the world, and their influence has by no means reached its zenith. We outsource an ever-greater part of our lives to devices and we get a lot in return: convenience, efficiency, entertainment, factual knowledge and influence. My impression is that we don't do this wittingly; changes take place and we are pulled along. One way of convincing ourselves that this is not the case is to simply welcome the developments with open arms, but this can quickly lead to naiveté.

The side effects are, like the positive effects, considerable. Any medication with such significant side effects would never reach the market. Perhaps it's not even correct to make a distinction between effects and side effects in the realm of digital media. Does this then give us a reason to reject it outright and to long

120

nostalgically for simpler times? No, it does not. And if negative thoughts occasionally rear their heads, we should take ourselves in hand and think positively: 'I live in an enormously exciting time in which the digital revolution has created possibilities no one had even thought of a hundred years ago. I am contemporary and I'm well aware of the one-sidedness of digital media. They constitute a power and a force under which I could succumb, but it's my task to redirect that which negatively influences the development of me and my children and turn it into a positive.'

What does this mean concretely? Here I can only offer general advice, but you can take these suggestions and apply them to your own lives. The time is past when we acted because someone else told us that we should.

Knowledge is power

Keep up to date with the subject of screen time and child development by reading books such as this one and looking in the bibliography for other works of interest. Read texts written by believers as well as sceptics. Try to understand the ever-changing situation and provide yourself with frameworks for your thinking and opinions, so that whenever you encounter a new gadget or application you are prepared to form a judgment. Show them how to make use of digital media in a positive manner while retaining their autonomy.

Monitoring content

If you don't want your children to encounter topics such as drinking, addiction, sex and violence in real life, they should not be allowed to encounter them in the virtual world of screens. For young children the boundary between real and virtual is paper thin and, as they get older, the virtual and real worlds overlap more and more.

Set a good example

If you don't want your children to sit endlessly in front of screens, don't do it yourself. If you want your children to explore the natural world, play sports or read a good book, then do those things yourself. Show them that we all have a place in offline networks too. The power of imitation is vast, and not only in children.

Counteracting negative effects

There are two ways to counteract the negative effects of screen time: by imposing limits and providing counterbalance.

IMPOSING LIMITS

There is nothing to prevent us setting up rules around our children's screen use as we do in other areas. Alcohol is not suitable for children and is not sold to children under the age of eighteen: it alters our brain chemistry and the damage is in part irreversible. There are arguments for applying the same rule to digital media, which also profoundly changes our children's brains, causing unused sections to disappear and others to become more dominant.

We could establish certain places in the home or times of day as screen-free zones: at the table, for example, in the living room or in the bedroom after bedtime. I have heard both parents and children talk enthusiastically about screen-free holidays during which there was suddenly more room for conversation, quality time with loved ones, discovery and adventure. If you're implementing this kind of change, bear in mind that people can be very grouchy for the first two or three days when we go through the process of kicking the habit. We'll experience withdrawal symptoms because the reward hormones that come with our screen-use habit and our 'I've-got-a-message' compulsion have been switched off. It's reassuring to find that even strong habits like these lose power after a few days – although they're not gone, which becomes clear when everyone slips back into their old habits after a holiday.

Share your experiences with other parents at school and with anyone who is involved in raising your children. Practise a few pithy sentences that clearly explain your opinions and why you feel the topic is so important. Do not be afraid to set limits on screen time when your children are visiting their friends, but do provide an alternative. Make your position regarding screen use clear to teachers, and if necessary, write up rules and regulations for screen time together with teachers and fellow parents.

PROVIDING COUNTERBALANCE

When I describe screen time as being one-sided, I'm referring to its tendency to encourage purely linear thinking, superficial observation and superficiality. But we can compensate for these negative influences by resolving to ensure our children also have plenty of meaningful experiences – for example, make sure children experience a moment of intense wonder every day. Wonder makes us open to the new, to the future, to miracles. After up to six weeks of experiencing wonder each day, focus on something else, such as respect, affection or compassion.

A spiritual perspective

My suggestions above of course also apply here, but what can be added? Do we parent differently when we become aware of the cooperation we can build with influences, forces and beings of the non-sensory world? The answer, I think, is both no and yes.

No because as contemporary people we cannot avoid finding ourselves in the midst of the revolution set in motion by digitisation. We must therefore connect with it, interact with it while remaining autonomous.

Yes because when we know what's at stake, either

through the study of anthroposophy, or another source of knowledge, or through our own experience, we can grow in both earnestness and enthusiasm.

Earnestness because we realise that the preservation of humanity, human freedom and development is at stake. Earnestness because we realise that in the digital world we encounter forces that far exceed our power and influence. Earnestness because we see thousands of children being spun into its web before our own eyes and by our own hands.

Enthusiasm because we are participants in a crucial phase in the history of humankind and the earth. Enthusiasm because we have been handed the means to safeguard our own inviolability and that of our children. Enthusiasm when we notice that we don't have to manage this task on our own; we are part of a network of like-minded people, a network quite as real as the digital web.

After these rather serious words, here are some practical suggestions:

1. Make a study of the similarities and differences between the workings of the human brain and nerves and those of modern electronic equipment.

2. Provide yourself with 'islands' where you can catch your breath: islands in time, islands in your home where you can quietly read, contemplate, meditate and pray.

3. Try not to view screens directly before going to bed: go for a walk, have a chat, meditate. If you fall asleep dazed by the screen, you will not have a productive or restful night.

4. Do not let go of any opportunity to discuss the true content of your children's virtual adventures – or any non-sensory experiences they may have.

And remember: *'Technology is neither good nor bad; nor is it neutral.'* [13]

Afterword

In this book I have tried to present a controversial topic in such a way that the facts and opinions interact without heaviness. The rapid developments in the realm of digital media mean that some data will already be out of date when this book is published. I would be grateful for any corrections, additions or practical examples and suggestions that readers can offer to aid my continuing research in this area.

Endnotes

Prelude

1. Steiner, R. and Wegman, I. *Extending Practical Medicine: Fundamental principles based on the Science of the Spirit*

   Anthroposophy is a philosophy developed by Rudolf Steiner (1861–1925), which upholds the belief that real freedom can only be obtained through individual spiritual development, gained through scientific study of the spiritual nature of humanity and the universe. He showed that such a path could inspire many cultural innovations in areas such as education, agriculture, medicine, architecture, science and the arts, which are still relevant and progessing today.

Chapter 1

2. 'Global village' is a term closely associated with Canadian-born philosopher of communication theory Marshall McLuhan.

Chapter 2

3. When we look at something in everyday life, both eyes focus on a single point. In front of a flat screen this cannot be done. In order to absorb the images, the eyes automatically lose their focus and the optical axes assume a parallel position. This is the cause of the typical TV stare. The intentional look that focuses on something in the real world or on a picture is replaced by a

way of looking that is determined by the moving image. It is a look without intention.

4. Conjunctivitis is an infection of the conjunctiva, the mucous membrane that covers the front of the eye and lines the inside of the eyelids. Conjunctivitis is popularly known as 'pinkeye' and can be caused by a cold or an allergy, but also by other sources of irritation in the eye.

5. Spinal disc herniation is a bulge in the intervertebral disc, in this context in the neck. This bulge can press on a nerve or on the spinal cord and cause pain or loss of function such as paralysis and/or loss of sensation.

6. The orthopaedic surgeon Piet van Loon and others described this phenomenon in the journal *Medisch Contact* (August 1, 2013), and it has been widely reported in the media worldwide.

7. Johann Wolfgang (von) Goethe (1749–1832) was a German writer and statesman, whose work includes poetry, plays, novels, memoirs, literary and aesthetic criticism, treatises on botany, anatomy and colour, and numerous notes on literature and science, letters and drawings.

8. Spitzer, M. *Digitale Demenz: Wie wir uns und unsere Kinder um den Verstand bringen* (Digital Dementia: How we Destroy the Minds of Ourselves and Our Children)

9. Thompson, C. *Smarter Than You Think: How Technology is Changing Our Minds for the Better*

10. Valkenburg, P.M. *Schermgaande jeugd. Over jeugd en media* (Screen youth: On Youth and Media)

11. Sigman, A. *Remotely Controlled. How Television is Damaging Our Lives*

12. van der Does, W. and van Straaten, P. *Zo ben ik nu eenmaal! Lastpakken, angsthazen en buiten- beentjes* (That's just the way I am! Troublemakers, scaredy-cats and mavericks)

13. Melvin Kranzenberg, cited by Clive Thompson in *Smarter Than You Think*, p. 247.

Chapter 3

14. Amongst others: Spitzer, M; Sigman, A; Wilmar, F.

15. An opera in four acts, first performed in 1859. The story of Faust who sells his soul to the devil is much older. Goethe wrote a play about Faust, in which the devil sometimes plays the role of exercising power and at other times more that of the seducer.

16. In the metamorphosis of plants, the flower appears as a new phenomenon when the polarity of leaf and stem cancel themselves out and together produce something new.

17. Every nerve, when stimulated, has a refractory period of a few milliseconds during which the nerve cannot be stimulated again. This also applies to the conductivity of visual stimuli.

18. See Spitzer, M. *Digitale Demenz*, Chapter 10.

19. The Dutch word *beeldscherm* combines these two into one word: image-screen

20. van Egmond, K. *Sustainable Civilization*

Chapter 4

21. Nikken, P., Pijpers, R. et al. *Iene Miene Media 2014. Een onderzoek naar mediagebruik door kleine kinderen* (A study on the use of media by young children), sponsored by *Mediawijzer* (Media guide). An English information page on Mediawijzer can be found via www.mediawijzer.net/about-mediawijzer-net.

22. Landsmeer, N. et al. 'Kind en beeldscherm: een te hecht koppel' (Child and screen: a team that's too close) in *Medisch Contact* 21

23. *Trouw* (June 7, 2014)

24. Furedi, F. *Paranoid Parenting. Why Ignoring the Experts May be Best for Your Child.*

25. An article based on the research appeared in the *Daily Mail*: www.dailymail.co.uk/news/article-462091/How-children-lost-right-roam-generations.html

Chapter 5

26. The phenomenological method starts from the notion that the essence of a phenomenon is given in its observation. We can reduce our perception to a sensory perception, but we can also observe carefully and let the phenomenon speak to us.

Chapter 6

27. Thomas Göbel has described this method in his book, *Die Quellen der Kunst. Lebendige Sinne und Phantasie als Schlüssel zur Architektur.* (Sources of Art: Living Senses and Fantasy as the Key to Architecture)

28. See Strauss, M. *Understanding Children's Drawings: Tracing the Path of Incarnation* and the chapter on children's drawings in Schoorel, E. *De eerste zeven jaar. Kinderfysiologie* (The First Seven Years: Children's Physiology)

Chapter 7

29. von Goethe, J. W. *The Fairy Tale of the Green Snake and the Beautiful Lily*

Chapter 8

30. Wilmar, F. *Over de invloed van radio en televisie op kleuters en jonge kinderen* (On the influence of radio and television on toddlers and young children)

31. Sound is in essence nothing but vibrations, and colour is essentially determined by the wavelength of light waves. Reducing a phenomenon to its physical characteristics can be called 'nothing butterism'. It stands in contrast to the notion of phenomenology.

32. To understand the world it's useful to divide it into twelve segments, and humans have a sense corresponding to each of these. For more on the twelve senses, see Albert Soesman, *Our Twelve Sense*, and the chapter on the senses in Edmond Schoorel, *De eerste zeven jaar: Ontwikkelingsfysiologie* (The First Seven Years: Children's Physiology).

33. This distinction is also presented in F. Wilmar's book (note 30).

34. *Trouw*, September 2, 2014

35. Thompson, C. *Smarter than You Think*

36. Spitzer, M. *Digitale Demenz*

Chapter 9

37. The Grey Men 'time savers' only exist through stealing time from humans and consuming it. Ende, M. *Momo*.

38. Sigman, A. *Remotely controlled*

39. See www.freerangekids.com in the US and www.scharrelkids.nl in The Netherlands.

Chapter 10

40. In 1997 the world chess champion Garry Kasparov was beaten by the supercomputer Deep Blue. Clive Thompson writes about this event in the first pages of *Smarter Than You Think*.

41. John von Neumann was one of the pioneers of computer technology. He worked in the US in the 1950s. Cited on p.15 of Steiner, R. *Der elektronische Doppelgänger und die Entwicklung der Computertechnik* (The electronic doppelganger and the development of computer technology) – a lecture given in November 1917 on the topic of electric machines, edited and with commentary by Andreas Neider.

42. The notion that only fixed DNA structures are inheritable has in recent years been called into question. Two professors from Erasmus University in Rotterdam explain this in an essay published in the *Volkskrant* of April 3, 2010: 'Parenting and environment can be inheritable like traits'. We are dealing in this context with 'epigenetics' – external environmental influences on genetic material. These influences can determine whether a hereditary trait (a piece of DNA) is switched off or on. Switched off it has no effect, switched on it does. The being switched off or on now also appears to be hereditary.

43. The results of a number of studies contradict each other. A recent study in Sweden (*Pathophysiology*, October 2014) shows a clearly increased risk of malignant brain tumours after long-term use of mobile phones. The younger the children are when they start using phones, the greater the risk. Other studies show no correlation ('Long-term Cell Phone Use Linked to Brain Tumor Risk', *Medscape*, Nov 13, 2014).

44. By 2006 giant industrial computer centres used as much energy as 2.5 million German households use in one year: 8.67 terawatt-hours (source: Borderstep Institut 2007). Between 2005 and 2010 energy used to power digital technology doubled, a trend that will continue in the years to come.

45. Two German physiologists carried out experiments on muscles and nerves from a dead frog to 'prove' that there are no forces at work in organisms other than common physical-chemical forces.

46. Dick Swaab is a famous Dutch neurobiologist, who wrote *We Are Our Brains: From the Womb to Alzheimer's.*

47. As indicated by two excellent Dutch-language books: Bos, A. *Hoe de stof de geest kreeg. De evolutie van het ik* (How Matter Got the Spirit: the Evolution of the Self) and Bos, A. *Mijn brein denkt niet, ik wel* (My Brain Does Not Think; I do).

48. de Saint-Exupéry, A. *The Little Prince*

Bibliography

Bilton, N. 'Steve Jobs was a low-tech parent', *New York Times*, http://nyti.ms/1qMfdln, USA, 2014.

Bos, A. *Hoe de stof de geest kreeg. De evolutie van het ik* (How matter got the spirit: the evolution of the self), Christofoor, The Netherlands, 2008.

—, *Mijn brein denkt niet, ik wel* (My brain does not think, I do), Christofoor, The Netherlands, 2014.

Dostoevski, F. 'The Grand Inquisitor' in *The Brothers Karamazov*.

Ende, M. *Momo*, Puffin Books, UK, 2009.

Furedi, F. *Paranoid Parenting. Why Ignoring the Experts May be Best for Your Child*, Bloomsbury, UK, 2008.

Göbel, T. *Die QueUen der Kunst. Lebendige Sinne und Phantasie als Schlüssel zur Architektur* (Sources of art: living senses and fantasy as the key to architecture), Verlag am Goetheanum, Germany, 1982.

—, *Natur und Kunst* (Nature and art), Freies Geistesleben, Germany, 1998.

Kurzweil, R. *The Singularity is Near*, Duckworth Overlook, UK, 2010.

Landsmeer, N. et al. 'Kind en beeldscherm: een te hecht koppel' (Child and screen: a team that's too close) in *Medisch Contact* 21, The Netherlands, May 22, 2014.

Large, M. *Who's Bringing Them Up? How to Break the TV Habit*, Hawthorn Press, 1990.

Lusseyran, J. *What One Sees Without Eyes*, Floris Books, UK, 1999.

—, *Against the Pollution of the I: On the Gifts of Blindness, the Power of Poetry, and the Urgency of Awareness*, New World Library, USA, 2016.

Postman, N. *Technopoly*, Vintage, UK, 1993.

—, *The End of Education: Redefining the Value of School*, Vintage, UK, 1996.

de Saint-Exupéry, A. *The Little Prince*, Egmont, UK, 2001.

Schoorel, E. *De eerste zeven jaar. Kinderfysiologie* (The first seven years: children's physiology), Christofoor, The Netherlands, 2014.

Sigman, A. *Remotely Controlled: How Television is Damaging Our Lives*, Vermilion, UK, 2007.

Soesman, A. *Our Twelve Senses: How Healthy Senses Refresh the Soul. An Introduction to Anthroposophy and Spiritual Psychology Based on Rudolf Steiner's Studies of the Senses*, Hawthorn Press, UK, 2001.

Spitzer, M. *The Mind Within the Net: Models of Learning, Thinking and Acting*, MIT Press, USA, 2000.

—, *Digitale Demenz: Wie wir uns und unsere kinder um den Verstand bringen*, Droemer Knaur, Germany, 2014.

Steiner, R. *Anthroposophical Leading Thoughts* (GA 26), Rudolf Steiner Press, UK, 1998.

—, *Theosophy* (GA 9).

—, *Knowledge of the Higher Worlds: How is it achieved?* (GA 10), Rudolf Steiner Press, UK, 2004.

Steiner, R. with commentary by Andreas Neider. 'Der elektronische Doppelgänger und die Entwicklung der Computer-technik' (The electronic doppelganger and the development of computer technology), lectures from November 1917, Futurum, Switzerland, 2012.

Steiner. R. and Wegman, I. *Extending Practical Medicine: Fundamental Principles Based on the Science of the Spirit*, Rudolf Steiner Press, UK, 1997.

Strauss. M. *Understanding Children's Drawings: Tracing the Path of Incarnation*, Rudolf Steiner Press, UK, 2007.

Swaab, D. *We Are Our Brains: From the Womb to Alzheimer's*, Allen Lane, UK, 2014.

Thompson, C. *Smarter Than You Think: How Technology is Changing Our Minds for the Better*, Collins, UK, 2014.

Valkenburg, P. M. *Schermgaande jeugd. Over jeugd en media* (Screen youth: youth and media), Prometheus-Bert Bakker, The Netherlands, 2014.

Van der Does, W. and Van Straaten, P. *Zo ben ik nu eenmaal! Lastpakken, angsthazen en buiten- beentjes* (That's just the way I am! Troublemakers, scaredy-cats and mavericks), Scriptum, The Netherlands, 2004.

Van Egmond, K. *Sustainable Civilization*, Palgrave Macmillan, UK, 2014.

Van Lommel, P. *Consciousness Beyond Life: The Science of the Near-Death Experience*, HarperOne, UK, 2011.

Weirauch, W. *Nature Spirits and What They Say: Interviews with Verena Stael von Holstein*, Floris Books, 2004.

Wilmar, F. annotated by Van Domburg, P. and Verbrugh, H. *Over de invloed van radio en televisie op kleuters en jonge kinderen* (On the influence of radio and television on toddlers and young children.), Society for Philosophy and Medicine, Rotterdam, The Netherlands, 2008.